The Samuel & Althea Stroum Lectures

IN JEWISH STUDIES

The Samuel & Althea Stroum Lectures

IN JEWISH STUDIES

The Yiddish Art Song
performed by Leon Lishner, basso,
and Lazar Weiner, piano
(stereophonic record album)

The Holocaust in Historical Perspective
by Yehuda Bauer

Zakhor: Jewish History and Jewish Memory
by Yosef Hayim Yerushalmi

Jewish Mysticism and Jewish Ethics
by Joseph Dan

The Invention of Hebrew Prose:
Modern Fiction and the Language of Realism
by Robert Alter

Recent Archaeological Discoveries and Biblical Research
by William G. Dever

Jewish Identity in the Modern World
by Michael A. Meyer

Jewish Identity in the Modern World

MICHAEL A. MEYER

University of Washington Press

SEATTLE & LONDON

Copyright © 1990 by the University of Washington Press
Printed in the United States of America
by Braun-Brumfield, Inc.
Designed by Audrey Meyer

Library of Congress Cataloging-in-Publication Data

Meyer, Michael A.
  Jewish identity in the modern world / Michael A. Meyer.
      p.   cm. — (The Samuel and Althea Stroum lectures in Jewish
  studies)
  Includes bibliographical references.
  ISBN 0-295-97000-6 (alk. paper)
      1. Jews—Identity—History.   2. Enlightenment.   3. Antisemitism.
  4. Zionism.   I. Title.   II. Series.
  DS143.M39   1990
  909'.04924—dc20   89-70707
                                                             CIP

ISBN 0-295-97000-6

The paper used in this publication meets the minimum requirements
of American National Standard for Information Sciences —
Permanence of Paper for Printed Library Materials, ANSI Z39.48–1984.

∞

The Samuel & Althea Stroum Lectures

IN JEWISH STUDIES

SAMUEL STROUM, businessman, community leader, and philanthropist, by a major gift to the Jewish Federation of Greater Seattle, established the Samuel and Althea Stroum Philanthropic Fund.

In recognition of Mr. and Mrs. Stroum's deep interest in Jewish history and culture, the Board of Directors of the Jewish Federation of Greater Seattle, in cooperation with the Jewish Studies Program of the Henry M. Jackson School of International Studies at the University of Washington, established an annual lectureship at the University of Washington known as the Samuel and Althea Stroum Lectureship in Jewish Studies. This lectureship makes it possible to bring to the area outstanding scholars and interpreters of Jewish thought, thus promoting a deeper understanding of Jewish history, religion, and culture. Such understanding can lead to an enhanced appreciation of the Jewish contributions to the historical and cultural traditions that have shaped the American nation.

The terms of the gift also provide for the publication from time to time of the lectures or other appropriate materials resulting from or related to the lectures.

Contents

✳

Acknowledgments

❧

THE CONCEPTS PRESENTED here were first worked out in seminars on modern Jewish identity that I have given for a number of years at the Hebrew Union College in Cincinnati. I am grateful to the scores of students in those seminars who helped sharpen my thinking, enabling me to formulate it easily in these lectures. Three of my colleagues in Cincinnati, Professors Barry Kogan, Benny Kraut, and Jonathan Sarna, read through the complete manuscript and made challenging suggestions, for which I am most grateful. My stay at the University of Washington was a glorious experience, thanks not only to marvelously sunny weather for most of it but also to the wonderful hospitality I enjoyed from faculty and staff. I am especially grateful to Dorothy Becker, who saw to my every need; to Rabbi Dan Bridge; and to my hosts Martin Jaffee, Jere Bacharach, Joel Migdal, John Haley, and Naomi Sokoloff. It was a special pleasure to spend time with Sam and Althea Stroum, whose extraordinary philanthropy is combined with an abiding interest in religion, humanities, and the arts. It has been gratifyingly easy to work with Naomi Pascal and Pamela Bruton at the University of Washington Press. My thanks to them for their interest in this book and their help in bringing it to publication.

Jewish Identity in the Modern World

Introduction

※

The Elusive Character
of Jewish Identity

LONG BEFORE THE WORD became fashionable among psychoanalysts and sociologists, Jews in the modern world were obsessed with the subject of *identity*. They were confronted by the problem that Jewishness seemed to fit none of the usual categories. Until the establishment of the state of Israel, the Jews were not a nation, at least not in the political sense; being Jewish was different from being German, French, or American. And even after 1948 most Jews remained nationally something other than Jewish. But neither could Jews define themselves by their religion alone. Few could ever seriously maintain that Judaism was, pure and simple, a religious faith on the model of Christianity. The easy answer was that Jewishness constituted some mixture of ethnicity and religion. But in what proportion? And was not the whole more than simply a compound of these two elements?

Martin Buber, surely one of the most profound of twentieth-century Jewish religious thinkers, argued that the Jews eluded all classification.[1] They were an anxiety-provoking specter to gentiles, a conundrum to themselves. Their uniqueness precipitated antisemitism

3

on the part of those unable to tolerate what could not be cubbyholed and a frenetic desire to fit into an accepted category on the part of Jews who could not bear the insecurity of being set apart. For Buber, the Jews' uniqueness was discernible only by the inner eye of faith and could be borne only as the yoke of the Kingdom of God. Jewish identity was no less elusive for Sigmund Freud, probably the most broadly influential Jew of the twentieth century. While from Freud's secular perspective, faith could play no role in determining his own Jewish self-understanding, he could no more than Buber simply equate Jewishness with ethnicity. It has been noted that the only instance in which Freud used the word *identity* in a more than incidental way occurs in an often-cited speech he wrote for delivery to his B'nai B'rith lodge in Vienna in 1926. There he admitted his irresistible attraction to Jews and Judaism on account of "many dark emotional forces, all the more potent for being so hard to grasp in words, as well as the clear consciousness of an inner identity, the intimacy (*Heimlichkeit*) that comes from the same psychic structure."[2] Like Buber, Freud found Jewish identity manifestly present in individual consciousness, but darkly beyond definition.

In recent decades it has not been the Jews alone who have fretted over their identity.[3] During the last generation the term has acquired a central position in psychological and social theory due, perhaps, to greater awareness of the dislocations in the relationship between individual and society that characterize the process of economic modernization and of the problems of preserving cultural continuity from one generation to another in the context of nontraditional societies. Much of this interest has, of course, been sparked by the work of Erik H. Erikson, who established identity as that category which links the

4

Introduction

psychological growth of individual persons with the norms of the society that they enter during adolescence. His writings have made psychoanalysts consider the broader tapestry of history and impelled historians to deal with the psychodynamics of individual development.

As Erikson's work gained increasing attention, other writers sought to apply it in clinical work, in social science, and in historiography. Identity was defined and redefined; its content and intensity were described in case histories and measured in the scales of public opinion surveys. Erikson himself had found the concept immensely fruitful but stubbornly elusive. He called identity "a term for something as unfathomable as it is all-pervasive."[4]

Like Jewish identity, identity as such is indeed a concept that allows of no easy categorization. Yet at least a preliminary understanding of the general concept must precede the analysis of its Jewish form. By drawing on Erikson, it is possible to delineate its contours. In these lectures I shall understand identity as referring to those totalities of characteristics which individuals believe to constitute their selves. Individual identity is built upon pre-adult identifications with persons close to the child, with their values and behavior patterns. As the individual becomes an adult these identifications must be integrated not only with one another but with the norms of the society in which the individual will play a role. This latter process represents "identity formation," an often troubled stage which, as Erikson showed, may result in prolonged adolescent crisis. Such crisis is especially likely to occur when there is a profound discontinuity between the earlier identifications, made within the more intimate family setting, and conflicting values that the individual encounters when moving beyond family into society. As we shall see, such discontinuities are crucial for understanding the identity conflict created at points of encounter between Jewishness and modernity. In psychoanalytic terms, the superego of the Jewish child, imbued with one set of sanctions mediated by parents as part of a Jewishly traditional society, is cast adrift in a historical setting that does not reinforce and may undermine them. There is, Erikson notes, a failure of expectations that can prove traumatic to identity formation.[5] The result is a sense of orphanhood[6] or, in social science terms, the creation of a psychologically uncomfortable cognitive dissonance between clashing sets of values.[7] Harmonizing ideologies appear in the attempt to reestablish continuity and relieve distress.

In premodern times the congruity between family and society prevented Jewish identity from becoming a problem. Parents implanted in children the same values that they had absorbed in growing up, values sanctioned by a spiritually self-sufficient Jewish society. Continuity prevailed across the generations. This is not to say that the transition from childhood to adulthood among premodern Jews was entirely smooth in each instance. Surely the psychodynamics of maturation created family crises even then, but they were contained within the framework of limited options available upon reaching adulthood. These might indeed include alternative ways of being Jewish, pietist or rationalist for example. But they were all within well-understood boundaries. The parentally implanted superego regularly made "a maximum of collective sense in terms of the ideals of the day."[8]

It is modernization that breaks down the barriers to the world outside the Jewish community and creates the choices that threaten continuity. From the perspective of Jewish identity, modernization is best understood as the historical process whereby increased exposure to non-

Introduction

Jewish ideas and symbols progressively erodes the given generational continuities, first in one location, then another, first among certain classes of Jews, then among others. Its product is Jewish modernity: the ongoing situation where internal continuity stands in potential or actual conflict with forces exterior to Jewish tradition. Put somewhat differently, a premodern, encompassing Jewish identity contracted to make room for other identity components, sometimes simply persisting alongside them, sometimes mingling with them freely. The relative influence of the Jewish component became subject to fluctuation, waxing or waning in relation to the new elements drawn from outside the Jewish sphere.

Writings on Jewish identity fall into three basic categories.[9] Social scientists have built complex models of Jewish identity structure and carried out extensive surveys in order to measure the intensity, shift, and direction of Jewish identification. Their analytic and quantitative studies have focused on the contemporary, with little consideration of longer range historical development. They are helpful in revealing current trends, less useful in understanding the contemporary situation in terms of its origins and the more general forces that impinge upon Jewish individuals and communities.[10] Another kind of literature has conveyed personal engagement. Prominent Jews have written about their own Jewishness. Some individuals have argued for the intensification of Jewish identity; others proposed ways in which it might be made richer in content and more effectively conveyed through Jewish education.[11] Such writings reflect the ongoing concern with Jewish survival and the recognition that Jewish identity represents its indispensable requisite. The third type of literature is historical. Mostly it has focused on particular

7

individuals or crucial periods in modern Jewish history. Usually less quantitative in approach than the sociological studies, it has interpreted those trends thought most decisive for a changing Jewish self-definition.

These lectures clearly fall into the third category. They are not principally concerned to establish a theory of Jewish identity; they are based on no original surveys. They also contain no reflections upon my own Jewish identity or suggestions for how Jewish identity might best be preserved and enhanced. However, unlike previous historical treatments, they attempt to span the entire field of Jewish modernity. Of course, they cannot in such brief compass make even brief reference to all instances of the ongoing encounter of Jewish identity with its competitors in the modern world. Historical sources here serve more as illustration than as integral elements of a chronological narrative. And they are drawn largely from areas of my own research or special interest. Nonetheless, my intent is to explicate a dynamics of Jewish identity in modernity that, with variations, I hold to be universally applicable.

These three lectures attempt to explain the operation and effect of the forces that I believe have shaped modern Jewish identity more than any others: enlightenment (the ongoing process), antisemitism, and the sense of Jewish peoplehood represented by Zion. Enlightenment beneficently drew Jews to identify with a larger world beyond the boundaries of Judaism. Antisemitism, in rejecting the Jews, acted ambiguously, both strengthening and weakening Jewish ties. Zion, although it has also had divisive effects, drew modern Jews together in support of a common goal. In varying combinations, these three forces compelled Jews to rethink and reevaluate their Jewish self-definition and the role of Jewishness in their lives. While

Introduction

each of them is linked to particular historical events, none has ceased to be influential. Thus all three lectures are historical in content and at the same time seek to understand the dynamics of external and internal forces that shape and reshape modern Jewish identity down to the present, and likely into the future as well.[12]

Enlightenment

❧

The Powerful Enticements
of Reason and Universalism

A S A PROPER NOUN *Enlightenment* refers to a particular intellectual movement in European history. Its
Jewish equivalent became known as the *Haskalah*. Although Enlightenment thinkers were not always friendly
to Jews, their movement influenced the Jewish turn to
broader horizons. My purpose here, however, is neither to
discuss the Enlightenment in relation to the Jews nor to
present a historical sketch of the Haskalah as it spread from
central Europe eastward to Russia. Instead, I shall principally be concerned with enlightenment in a generic sense,
as a force operating upon individual Jews and Jewish communities, engendering various responses and reflected in
differing forms of Jewish identity. Thus it is the content
and effect of enlightenment that matters here, not its rep-
resentatives or organized forms. That content I take to be
composed principally of two interrelated elements: reason
and universalism. They are interrelated because reason implies a universal community of rational persons, and universalism, in turn, requires a common, rational basis of
discourse. Viewed thus broadly, the influence of enlight-

Enlightenment

enment has been significant in Jewish history for more than two centuries.

Enlightenment has been both an erosive force, undermining Jewish identity in its premodern form, and a constituent element of its modern varieties. On the one hand, it has challenged the Jewish doctrine of supernatural revelation and the Jews' religious or ethnic exclusivism. But on the other, it has become integral in the identities of nearly all modern Jews; few Jews today still seek to exclude it.

In order better to understand the numerous ways in which enlightenment has affected modern Jewish identity, it will be useful to begin with a brief consideration of premodern Jewish identity. Here it seems necessary to note immediately that rationalism and universalism were, of course, not entirely foreign to Jewish consciousness even before modern times. There is a rich tradition of Jewish philosophy extending back to Philo of Alexandria and down through the Middle Ages. Jews never repudiated the universalism of the biblical prophets. But for various reasons, not the least of them exclusion and persecution, Jewish communities before the modern period had largely neglected this heritage, stressing instead their own divinely ordained separation and superiority.

Drawing upon the work of Jacob Katz,[1] we can easily note the elements of exclusiveness that went into the premodern Jewish identity as it was passed on through the generations. At its heart was the firm belief that the Jews were God's chosen people, that they stood in a special relationship to God, that the persecution they suffered in exile was due only to their own sinfulness, and that upon full repentance they would be restored to a glorious existence in their own land. A messiah from their stock would rule the nations of the earth. Jewish children were imbued with belief in a sharp dichotomy between Jews and gentiles. The former were deemed pure, children of the covenant, while the latter were called impure and uncircumcised. One was not to regard them highly or imitate their actions.[2] When rage at their persecutors welled up within them and when censors did not prevent them from writing freely, medieval Jews referred to Christians as idolaters, to their churches as houses of abomination, and to their saviour as the hanged one.[3] Seen in purely empirical terms, Judaism had been vanquished by its triumphant daughter religions: Christianity in the West and Islam in the East. But in the superempirical perspective of faith, the Jews remained dearest to God.

Physical segregation, sometimes welcomed by the Jews themselves, and badges imposed by gentiles to mark them as Jews reinforced these feelings of exclusiveness. So did Jewish law, which prohibited Jews from drinking gentile wine and eating gentile food, allowed them to take interest from non-Jews but not from Jews, and valued strict observance of the sabbath above saving the life of a gentile on that day. There was no neutral ideological ground upon which Jew and gentile could meet, no religion of humanity that they shared. Individuals were wholly the one or the other. Conversion was the only pathway out of the ghetto. Within its walls, clear models of Jewish identity were instilled in the home, in the school, in the community. There were no significant discontinuities, no occasions for severe crises of identity.

The medieval Jewish community left little room for individuality. It imposed its norms sternly upon each child growing up and upon each adult. Haym Soloveitchik has shown the extreme form this took among the Hasidim of medieval Germany.[4] Here conformity was demanded not

Enlightenment

only in act but in sentiment, with dire divine punishment envisaged for those who failed to live up to the community ideal. The medieval Hasidim were not averse to burning books that conveyed a conflicting message and to encouraging all members of the community to enforce the collective will on each individual. Building fences inside fences, they regarded even non-Hasidic Judaism as threatening religious purity. The gentile world lay yet further away, beyond the outermost barrier.[5]

In some places Jewish exclusivism receded during the late Middle Ages, but only slowly and incompletely. The more tolerant attitude of the late thirteenth-century Provençal rabbi Menahem Ha-Meiri, who distinguished Muslims and Christians from idolaters, did not become dominant for Ashkenazi Jewry during his own time or for centuries thereafter. The new Hasidic movement, born in eighteenth-century eastern Europe and still very much alive today, perpetuated the sharp dichotomy between the Jewish and gentile worlds. One of its most central texts gives that dichotomy metaphysical status when, drawing upon the Jewish mystical tradition, it declares that since the souls of the nations of the world emanate from the realm of evil, they are inherently incapable of doing good for its own sake.[6] In the nineteenth century, the leading Hungarian rabbi Moses Sofer cautioned his descendants to stay far from would-be modernizers and to read none of their writings. Rather, they should confine their studies to the traditional texts and commentaries, while keeping their names unchanged, their dress traditional, and their language that of the Jews.[7] Still today a tiny segment of the Jewish community rejects enlightenment as an anti-Jewish intrusion and in the extreme instance crosses the border from religious exclusivism into chauvinism or racism.[8] The vast majority of Jews, however, have incorporated

13

enlightenment into their identities, making room for it alongside their Jewish legacy or even harmonizing the two. How did this come about?

I t was in seventeenth-century Holland that the first major conflict between community-enforced Jewish identity and modern individuality occurred. The Sephardi Jews of Amsterdam had adopted some of the rigid religious authoritarianism of the Iberian Catholic environment from which they had fled. Like the Inquisition, they possessed little tolerance for dissent. Yet their own identity was uncertain. Some had been Marranos, secretly identifying as Jews but possessing only imperfect knowledge of Judaism and unable to practice it fully. In Amsterdam they asserted their Jewishness without dread of persecution, but out of an apparent lingering insecurity, they feared heresy as a force that could undermine their newly won redefinition as normative Jews.

Uriel Acosta had himself been a Marrano in Portugal before he arrived in Amsterdam in the second decade of the seventeenth century. But his return to Judaism was troubled from the start. A startlingly independent personality, whose Jewish identity was not transmitted naturally in childhood, he came to active Jewish identification out of a growing conviction that Judaism was the true faith. His continued adherence to it depended on whether that conviction could be sustained. Mistakenly, he had come to believe that Judaism was simply the faith of the Hebrew Bible. Once he discovered that biblical laws and tenets had been considerably altered and expanded by the rabbis, he found himself at odds with Amsterdam Jewry. When he persistently rejected rabbinic Judaism in belief and practice, they excommunicated him. Unable to find a way of

Enlightenment

living both within the Jewish community and in harmony with his conscience, he finally committed suicide.[9]

Acosta is of particular interest for the study of Jewish identity. Like the talented intellectuals Erikson has described, who undergo a prolonged identity crisis in the attempt to achieve a consistent worldview, Acosta was a man with little tolerance for contradiction. His inner need for consistency drove him first from the New Testament to the Old and finally to a rejection of all revelation in favor of natural law alone. His last choice was for the coherence provided by untrammeled reason as the sole guide for life. Baruch Spinoza, who lived just after Acosta in Amsterdam, followed a similar path. For him, as well, Jewish identity gave way before a larger attachment to the community of all rational persons, even though that community had as yet no basis in social reality. Spinoza, too, was placed under the ban.

Neither Acosta nor Spinoza left Judaism for another faith community. To their contemporaries they were heretics, men whose convictions pushed them out of a Judaism that could not tolerate their deviation. Yet paradoxically, Acosta—and especially Spinoza—became models of Jewish identity for later Jewish intellectuals.[10] It was precisely their nonconformity that appealed to those Jews of subsequent generations who began to define their own Jewishness in terms of marginality and the insights that it offered. Late in life Freud referred to himself as "an old Jew, but an infidel one"; the philosopher Walter Kaufmann called his religion "the faith of a heretic"; and the Marxist Jewish intellectual Isaac Deutscher chose to identify with a whole chain of Jewish heretical tradition that ran from Elisha ben Abuyah in ancient times through Spinoza, Heine, and Marx, to Rosa Luxemburg, Trotsky, and Freud.[11] But Acosta and Spinoza in their day remained socially isolated. They stood alone outside the Jewish consensus. Not until a century later did a movement that enjoyed growing support begin within Jewish communities to broaden identifications, extending them beyond the boundaries of Judaism.

It was the European Enlightenment of the eighteenth century that initiated the process undermining Jewish exclusivism.[12] Despite the ambivalence of Enlightenment thinkers toward Jews and their all but unanimous condemnation of Judaism, the universal, rational categories in which they thought drove them to include Jews within the fellowship of humanity. Natural religion, the religion of reason, was a faith underlying both Judaism and Christianity. As the environment became less hostile, and as Jews and Christians came into closer social contact, those Jews most exposed to gentiles and their ways began to identify themselves not only as Jews but also as German or French, as Europeans, or simply as enlightened human beings. Jewish identity contracted to make room for new elements absorbed from the outside world. The result was widening intergenerational and intracommunity conflict. No longer was there a clear consensus. No longer was the transition from generation to generation an easy one. And no longer was it a matter of an occasional "heretic." Rather, for increasing numbers of Jews then coming of age, Jewish identity ceased to be a natural, unselfconscious framework for their lives. As enlightenment penetrated one class of Jews after another and one community after another, Jewish identity became problematic. Which elements of the self now remained Jewish? Was one principally a Jew and secondarily a European, or vice versa? Identity crisis became a recurrent feature in the generational transmission of Jewishness. Wherever enlightenment penetrated, it brought self-consciousness and, especially for intellectuals, the need to achieve self-definition.

The new identifications called into question some of the old ones. For Moses Mendelssohn, who managed to live both as a traditional Jew and as a man of the European Enlightenment, the latter component of his identity sometimes jostled the former. As a rationalist he could not believe that demons attacked Jewish corpses before burial; as a European he could find no value in traditional Jewish dress; and as a Germanophile he found the Yiddish language to be a corrupting influence. But mostly he solved the problem of potential conflict by separating and narrowing his Jewish identity while leaving it basically intact. His Jewishness became a matter of private conscience. Unlike the Sephardi authorities of Amsterdam, he would not impose his own convictions on anyone else. Neither church nor state, he believed, should act coercively in matters of religion. Personally, he could live at peace in two spheres, for Judaism and reason, Judaism and European culture, did not conflict. His religion, as he interpreted it, possessed no superrational dogmas, and it was fully tolerant of divergent faith communities. What set the Jews apart—and constituted their special identity—was for Mendelssohn preeminently the law that God had revealed to them at Sinai. It governed their actions but not their thoughts.

Yet although, unlike the law, rational religion was not for Jews alone, it was in Mendelssohn's view a particular legacy of Judaism to have propagated it, and its continued advocacy constituted a Jewish vocation. Jews were chosen by Providence "to call wholesome and unadulterated ideas of God and His attributes continuously to the attention of the rest of mankind."[13] Mendelssohn thus set forth the idea of the "mission of Israel," which became one of the principal components of modern Jewish identity in its essentially religious variety. Judaism was the enlightened religion par excellence. To be a Jew was therefore not to preserve the fragments of an outworn identity hopelessly at odds with enlightenment. Just the opposite was true: rational religion was the legacy of Judaism, not yet fully absorbed by non-Jews. Jewish identity became focused outward. One was a Jew because one had a mission to the non-Jew, a mission that not only was in harmony with modernity but could help to shape it.

Mendelssohn, and those who followed him, defined Jewish identity primarily in religious terms. To be a Jew now came to mean belonging to a religious denomination, more or less like the Christian ones. Jewish identity was expressed by avowing beliefs and practicing rituals. The unit of Jewish continuity was the community of faith. For the modern Orthodox the Jewish religion was eternal and hence could easily serve as the vehicle of Jewish identity from generation to generation. But religious reformers faced a more difficult situation when they thinned the ethnic strand of continuity, for the Jewish religion, as they conceived it, had changed in the past and would continue to change. Aside from its universalist credo of ethical monotheism, Liberal Judaism offered no permanent mooring to which Jewish identity could be made fast. Its proponents were forced to understand Jewishness in its particularity as ever developing along with the evolution of the Jewish religion.

Mendelssohn served most fully as an identity model for modern Jewish Orthodoxy. Like Mendelssohn, Samson Raphael Hirsch, the progenitor of Neo-Orthodoxy in nineteenth-century Germany, was a man of European culture and broader identifications. For generations of mod-

Enlightenment

ern Orthodox Jews in Germany and elsewhere, Hirsch's writings successfully neutralized the dangers inherent in enlightenment by arguing that Jewish religion and contemporary culture could exist compartmentally side by side. It was simply necessary to insist on the primacy of revelation at every point of theological conflict. Like Mendelssohn, Hirsch remained observant of the law and preached to the Jews their mission of bringing religious truth to the gentiles. But other modern religious Jews deviated from Orthodoxy and thereby withdrew from Mendelssohn's shadow. For them critical historical thought eroded faith that both the Written and Oral Law had been presented to Moses at Sinai. Conservative spirits, like Zacharias Frankel, were able to harmonize historical criticism with revelation by historicizing the rabbinic literature while leaving the Written Torah untouched as the directly revealed word of God. As far as we know, cognitive dissonance never disturbed Frankel's apparently tranquil soul. He was able to see himself and his generation as a link in the chain of halakhic development. Abraham Geiger, the religious reformer, presents a sharply contrasting picture of severe identity crisis. Emerging from an Orthodox home into a German university setting that challenged the traditions which had nurtured him, Geiger long and painfully struggled to achieve a Jewish identity into which he could incorporate commitment to the methods and findings of historical science. Scholarship demanded critical distance, looking at Judaism from the outside. But being a Jew and, in his case, a rabbi required inner identification with the totality of the Jewish experience. Eventually, Geiger was able to integrate both roles into his life and help to create a form of Judaism in which faith did not set bounds to science.[14]

For other Jews, especially after Geiger's time, the religious component of Jewish identity gave way entirely before the scientific ideals of scholarship. Learning, which had been a Jewish value when applied in a traditional manner to religious texts, became an independent characteristic of Jewish identity. Studying remained a form of Jewish expression, even when the method of study was critical and the purpose to test one's acumen or to write a work of scholarship rather than to discern God's will.[15] And finally, learning became Jewish regardless even of its content. For many Jews the serious study of any worthy subject became a way of being Jewish.

But intellectual challenges were not the only ones that assailed Jewish identity. An increasing number of the young felt estranged from their fellow Jews no less than they felt alienated from Jewish tradition. Enlightenment not only made their ancestors' beliefs and practices unacceptable to them, it distanced them from parents and relatives and reduced their sense of oneness with the Jewish people as a whole, most of whom remained as yet unenlightened. In the writings of enlightened German Jews around the turn of the nineteenth century there are at least three instances in which the author undertakes an elaborate classification of the Jews of his time according to degrees of enlightenment.[16] Each author identifies himself with the small group that he regards as the truly enlightened. The remaining Jews, clinging to superstitions or—in extreme reaction—forsaking Judaism for libertinism, are not objects of identification. The range of Jewish social identity narrows as growing differences among Jews make full identification possible only with a smaller group within the Jewish community. For the enlightened Jews it is their fellow enlightened; for the traditionalists it is those who have stood steadfast with them in opposing the intrusion of alien values.

Enlightenment

This fragmentation required the use of new designations. Enlightened Jews who had emancipated themselves
from rabbinic law and customs, reducing the textual basis
for their identity to the Bible, chose such designations as
Mosaist. A broad spectrum of Jews, including the modern
Orthodox, found that they did not want to call themselves
Jews, because that term not only was used contemptu-
ously by gentiles but was associated with their exclusivism
in the premodern world. They chose *Israelite* or *Hebrew*
instead, terms that were used in the title of both Reform
and Orthodox Jewish newspapers in various countries. To
separate themselves from Reformers, traditional Jews also
required a more specific and positive term than Orthodoxy. They chose *Torah-true,* by which they meant loyalty to the full twofold revelation of Written and Oral
Law.

Aside from the home, it was the school in which the
child made the identifications that were shaped into personal identity. Not surprisingly, education was from the
beginning a principal concern of the maskilim, the Jewish
enlighteners. In altering the curriculum of the Jewish
school to embrace secular as well as Jewish studies, they
inculcated values that lay outside Judaism. In giving the
students teachers who stood with one foot in the Jewish
community and the other in the non-Jewish world, the
educators displayed personal models very different from
those presented by the conventional teacher of small children, the melamed. The combination of traditional home
and modern schooling generated identity conflicts that
could not easily be resolved. Only after Jewish homes too
began to integrate non-Jewish culture did this gap between
parents and children, characterizing the first generation of
enlightenment (whenever and wherever enlightenment
first made inroads), cease to be so severe.

Perhaps the most insidious value that European culture set against Jewish tradition was not scientific truth but beauty. Mendelssohn himself had developed an interest in aesthetics. His successors carried it further, studying the Bible, for example, as a work of extraordinary literary merit rather than simply as a religious text. But although an appreciation for beauty, especially in relation to a religious purpose, was not entirely absent from any period of Jewish history, its veneration was Greek, not Hebrew. As enlightenment brought Jews to aesthetic awareness, they often saw themselves compelled to choose between Hellenism and the strict moralism of Jewish tradition. The poet Heinrich Heine felt this conflict intensely, and for most of his life chose to emulate the handsome young men of Greece rather than the stern patriarchs of ancient Israel. Later generations of Jews in eastern Europe were similarly attracted by the alien ideal of beauty. The Hebrew poet Hayyim Nahman Bialik described the fatal allure of natural beauty to the yeshiva student; the poet Saul Tchernichovsky imagined himself venerating the statue of Apollo, the Greek god of handsome masculinity. Even if Jewish secular poets and artists could, like Jewish rationalists, find some precedent for their artistic enterprise in the Jewish past, it was far more difficult for them to overcome the conflict with a tradition deeply suspect of art for its own sake and to absorb aesthetic values into Jewish identity.

Not always did modern Jews reach out willingly to acquire enlightenment. Sometimes it was forced on them. Especially in the German states, governments often made political emancipation conditional upon the Jews' giving up various forms of self-exclusion. They would grant equality only once Jews spoke the language of the land, possessed some secular education, and identified themselves fully with their environment. Some Jews, who

Enlightenment

were themselves enlightened, thereupon urged enlightenment on their coreligionists, arguing the value of the political reward. But traditionalists, wary of the assimilation
that would follow upon both enlightenment and political
integration, could find no merit in the argument. Patriotism, they recognized, represented a diminution of Jewish
identity and especially of its powerful messianic component. Indeed, for many Jews in the West, the state and
nation soon became the dominant objects of identification.
In Germany, the relation between German and Jewish
identity elements was tellingly expressed in the title German Jews gave their large defense organization, founded
in 1893. They called it the Central Association of German
Citizens of the Jewish Faith.

E ven in Tsarist Russia, where onerous restrictions on
the Jews were altered from time to time but never
removed entirely, some maskilim favored identification
with the Russian people and its rulers. Grasping at straws,
they urged fellow Jews to believe in the good intentions of
the regime and in the willingness of the gentile Russian to
call the Jew his brother. But the reality of rejection, which
ever and again punctured such illusions, prevented east
European Jews from ever being able to consider themselves fully Russians, Poles, or Ukrainians.

Thus the Russian Haskalah was more focused inward
than its German predecessor. Rather than defining Jewishness narrowly in religious terms to make room for
other identifications, it sought to bring the outside world
inside an expanded Jewish sphere. But that enlarged Jewish sphere would look very different. In one of the Russian
Haskalah's earliest programmatic statements, *Te'udah be-
Yisrael* (A mission in Israel),[17] Isaac Baer Levinsohn urged
a transformation whereby Jewish schools would teach the

sciences and the languages of the lands in which Jews lived along with Hebrew presented according to its grammatical rules. Only the few who required professional expertise as rabbis would study Talmud. The new Jew, educated in this manner, Levinsohn showed, would not represent a sharp break with the past but only embody traditions that were well precedented, especially among the Sephardim. The medieval philosophers Saadia and Maimonides, for example, were models of the rationalism that Levinsohn was propagating. Thus enlightenment was not a departure from Judaism but merely the substitution for presently dominant values of others drawn from its past. In retaining attachment to Hebrew, moreover, the more moderate of the east European maskilim sought to preserve an ethnic bond that rapidly disintegrated in the West. Levinsohn and later writers were fully cognizant of its role in uniting Jews everywhere. Unlike the Jewish religious reformers in Germany, they left worship services in Hebrew. They also differed in not copying Christian practices—at least in part because the Russian Orthodox church, unlike the Protestants in Germany, did not present an attractive model of religious modernization. It was only the excessive rigor with which Jewish law was applied and the narrowness of a religious leadership that denounced all secular learning that the Russian maskilim excoriated with bitter sarcasm. Their ideal was *dat im da'at,* religion together with (secular) knowledge, both of them within the Jewish orbit.

Yet in eastern Europe, as well, enlightenment wrought havoc, for secular knowledge not only expanded intellectual horizons, it presented new perspectives from which the beliefs that one held and the customs that one practiced as a Jew looked irrational or ugly. The result was a step-by-step process in which the sancta of Judaism were desac-

Enlightenment

ralized and ultimately rejected. The role model for the Jewish boy had been the *talmid ḥakham*, the scholar of sacred texts; for the girl the *eshet ḥayil*, the faithful wife and mother. Enlightenment introduced new models: for men, especially the physician, later also the industrialist; for some Jewish women, the pharmacist. Talmud study was not merely displaced in the curriculum, it became an object of derision along with the manner in which it was taught. The rationalistic scalpel at first cut away only superstitions: belief in demons and the use of amulets. But once the incision was made, there was no holding back the knife. Rabbinic legends, then rabbinic laws, and finally biblical laws were stripped away one by one. As traditional belief waned, the practices that it sanctioned fell into neglect. Once the Haskalah became more radical, its adherents gave up not only the garments that marked them as Jews but also the phylacteries (tefillin), strict observance of the sabbath, and finally the dietary laws (kashrut). The spread of religious negligence seems to have progressed more rapidly among men than women, the latter preserving traditions within the more pervasively Jewish atmosphere of the home, in which they spent a larger portion of their daily lives. As men visited the synagogue ever more rarely, it ceased to serve them as a source for news of the larger world outside the Jewish community. In place of the conversation on secular topics (*shmues*) conducted there on weekdays and filtered through Jewish concerns, non-Jewish newspapers became the purveyors of information, bringing their own perspective to contemporary events.

Perhaps the greatest weakness of the Russian Haskalah was its inherent instability. For many maskilim it was not a destination but only a station on a continuing odyssey. It undermined the old way of life without providing a sat-

isfactory new one. Y. L. Gordon, one of the most prominent of Russian maskilim, came to the sad recognition
that the Haskalah was the ideology of a single generation.[18] The children of the maskilim went on to leave
the Jewish heritage behind altogether. No longer believ-
ers, substituting the Russian language for Hebrew, their
Jewish identity became vestigial. In her memoirs Pauline
Wengeroff well expressed the transitional character of the
middle generation by citing premonitions that her mother
used to express: "Two things I can say for sure: I and my
generation will certainly live and die as Jews; our grand-
children will surely not live and die as Jews. Only what
our children will become—that I cannot guess."[19]

What happened to that third generation that went beyond the Haskalah's objective of enlightenment within the
Jewish sphere? Those Russian and Polish Jews most concerned for their careers often converted to Christianity as
their similarly motivated coreligionists had begun to do
earlier in the West. Some were drawn to alien ideologies.
They became positivists, substituting a universal, antimeta-
physical, and practically oriented philosophy for both religion and literary culture. Or they turned to socialism, in
which they found a cause demanding the same commitment that traditional Judaism had imposed upon the premodern generations. Only continued persecution of Jews
could occasionally revive vestigial sympathies in Jewish
radicals like the Menshevik leaders Pavel Axelrod and
Julius Martov.[20]

The most extreme among Jewish socialists regarded socialism as an identity that could not be harmonized with
Judaism. Either one identified with the Jewish people and
its religion or with the international proletariat and its rejection of all religion as simply a veil masking the privi-
leged status of the wealthy. Jewish socialists of this kind

Enlightenment

rejected their Jewish origins or regarded them as insignificant. Some were even willing to accept the negative stereotypes of Jews promulgated by their fellow socialists. Rosa Luxemburg neither identified as a Jew nor displayed any particular concern for the persecutions suffered by fellow Jews. She was a consistent and uncompromising internationalist. Leon Trotsky too denied any Jewish loyalty, though he at least recognized that Jews were especially vulnerable to their enemies. Perhaps the most extreme in rejecting Jewish identity were the Jewish *narodniki,* Jews who romantically associated themselves with the cause of the Russian country masses. Unlike the Jewish Marxists, they did not flee their particular Jewish identity for a universal one that embraced and superseded all others. They played at being what they patently were not: intimates of the simple, Russian Orthodox peasants. Sometimes they were shocked to discover that although they had forsworn their Jewish identity, the peasants they sought to serve nonetheless regarded them—negatively— as Jews. Later, during the early years of the Soviet Union, the Jewish Sections of the Communist Party had little success in transforming Jewish identity into a religionless, Yiddishist form of proletarian culture. The Bolshevik leadership remained fundamentally unsympathetic to any form of Jewish separatism, and few Russian Jews could wax enthusiastic over a Jewishness whose content was mostly at odds with traditional Jewish values.[21]

In the United States, too, the universalism and rationalism of enlightenment drew Jews to the periphery of Jewish identity and some of them beyond it. During the latter part of the nineteenth century the American Reform movement entered its "classical" phase. Ritual observance in Reform synagogues and homes diminished in accordance with the conviction that advanced religion was based on ethics, not symbolic acts. Particularizing rituals, which tended to reinforce Jewish identity, such as blowing the ram's horn at the New Year, building booths on the Feast of Tabernacles, and observing dietary laws, were all but abandoned. To be a Jew in the sense of classical Reform Judaism meant to be an adherent of ethical monotheism, a faith that derived from the Hebrew prophets but was not meant for Jews alone. Jewish identity was being part of a community that cherished commitment to the universalistic ideal of a single God worshipped by a united humanity. One remained a Jew to propagate that ideal.

But was a particular identity indeed necessary to advance the universal goal? Felix Adler, the son of a Reform rabbi, thought not. In 1876 he founded the New York Society for Ethical Culture, which soon attracted hundreds of peripheral Jews to its ranks. Adler simply followed the impetus of enlightenment to what he saw as its logical conclusion. His commitment to reason drew him to a Kantianism that left no room for a personal God but only for an impersonal moral Power. His universalism led him to criticize Reform Judaism's adherence to the mission of Israel as a form of chauvinism no better than the ancient chosen people concept. To be sure, Adler did not virulently reject his Jewish identity; he was proud of his ancestry. But its personal meaning was limited to origins. Like the Jewish socialists in Europe, he identified with humanity in general, not the Jews in particular. In the present, Judaism was a vestige, not an active force; it was destined to lose its distinctiveness within the sea of humanity. The future, he believed, lay in an eclectic religion beyond all religious particularisms, those of Christianity and other faiths no less than those of Judaism. And there was no compelling reason to postpone that future. Mixed

Enlightenment

marriages, like those of his own children, were a step in the right direction.[22]

Enlightenment thus manifested itself as a force that could draw Jews further and further away from Jewish identity, across the territory where one was a Jew and at the same time something else as well (European, German, Kantian, socialist), to the border where Jewish identity became vestigial or disappeared entirely. Yet in the border regions countervailing forces arose that sometimes reversed the trajectory. In the succeeding lectures we shall analyze the two most important such forces: antisemitism and Jewish nationalism. But often the Jewish religion also played a large role in such processes of reorientation. During the last two generations the American Reform movement has sought to recapture religious traditions that it had earlier rejected as primitive or inappropriate to the West. At least in part this counterthrust in Reform Judaism has been propelled by an awareness that when enlightenment is fully internalized, it leaves so little room for the specifically Jewish that the residue is insufficient for generational transmission. Similarly, some individual Jews who seemed furthest removed from Jewishness have attached themselves to religious Orthodoxy, occasionally turning their backs on enlightenment with a vengeance. These *ba'ale teshuvah* (repentants) have become an ever more common phenomenon both in Israel and in the United States.[23] Not always, however, is return from the border regions easy or complete. The histories of two prominent individuals will illustrate its complexity.

The middle-class parents to whom Vladimir Medem was born in 1879 in Minsk regarded their Jewish origins as a misfortune. They tried as best they could to hide this inherited stigma, of which they were greatly ashamed. At birth Vladimir was baptized into the Russian Orthodox church. His parents converted from Judaism later—but to Lutheranism. Yet family acquaintances continued to be Jews or ex-Jews, as was often the case among converts from Judaism. Vladimir's closest friends in school were invariably the Jewish students, who found one another more out of a felt affinity than on account of antisemitism, of which they apparently experienced very little in school. When he became a student at the university in Kiev, Medem began to envy the sense of group identity enjoyed by the Jewish students there. They had a "home"; he did not. He soon felt what he later called a "homesickness" or a "nostalgia" for Jewishness. He began an odyssey from the border back to the center. It was accomplished by no sudden leap but gradually, by degrees, almost unconsciously. "I can only identify the two terminal points," he wrote, "my childhood years when I considered myself a Russian; and the later period, the time of adulthood, when I considered myself a Jew. Both points encompassed a whole series of years during which I changed slowly, imperceptibly."[24] Medem declared his nationality as Jewish and began to learn Yiddish. He became one of the principal intellectual leaders of the Bund, the socialist association of Jewish workers. Unlike Luxemburg and Trotsky, Medem had intense and special feelings for his fellow Jews that prompted him to identify deeply with the lot of the Jewish workers and to fight for their cause. Yet Medem—and the Bund in general—remained more universal than particular in orientation. And his Jewish sentiments were always in tension with his devotion to the larger aims and strategies of the socialist revolution.

Unlike Medem's, Franz Kafka's family was not seeking to escape the onus of Judaism through conversion. They

Enlightenment

were comfortably established in Prague and, like many German-speaking Jews there, marked their Jewishness by occasional, halfhearted appearances in the synagogue. This attenuated Jewish identity did not transfer from father to son. The young Kafka, deeply resentful of his father in many respects, castigated him also for passing on a religious heritage so insincerely held that "I could not understand how one could do anything better with the stuff of such a faith than to get rid of it as quickly as possible. In fact getting rid of it seemed to me the most respectful thing one could do."[25] Kafka's odyssey, which eventually brought him to a much more intense Jewish identity than that of his parents, thus began with rejection. To become an identifying Jew, Kafka was forced to regain territory on his own. His positive relation to Judaism came after adolescence and from outside his home. In a way, gaining a meaningful Jewish identity was a rebellion against his upbringing.[26]

Kafka found his way to Jewish affirmation by identifying with those Jews least admired by his family and their friends: the *Ostjuden,* the Jews from eastern Europe. He became closely acquainted with a group of Yiddish actors at the Cafe Savoy and once gave a speech introducing a program of readings from Yiddish literature. He visited the home of a Hasidic rabbi. Among these east Europeans he found a spontaneity and genuineness lacking among German Jews. He also joined a circle of Zionist intellectuals whose influence was responsible for his becoming a Zionist and studying Hebrew. Yet like Medem, Kafka remained to some extent an outsider among his fellow Jews. On one occasion he wondered to his diary whether he really had anything in common with them. Interpreters of Kafka's novels have argued that his lonely protagonists reflect the situation of the rootless Jew in the modern world. But Kafka does not specifically identify them as Jews. For what is significant about his characters is that they bear the universal burden of modernity. That burden of existential loneliness separates the individual from all collective identities. Even as he became a Jew, Kafka remained apart.

The examples of Medem and Kafka, which could easily be multiplied, illustrate how individual motivation could lead to the repossession of Jewish identity, albeit in a new and individualized form, when its transmission through the generations had ceased or been impaired. But they illustrate also the continuing impact of enlightenment upon all those who do not withdraw from it to an intellectual ghetto or to an ideological extreme. Its effect may be to enhance the sense of human solidarity, as in the case of Medem, or of the common lot of individual separation, as was true for Kafka. But it is an ongoing force that persistently draws Jews to look beyond their Jewishness even as they seek to absorb it alongside of or within their particular identity as Jews.

Antisemitism

❦

The Ambiguous Effects
of Exclusion and Persecution

As ENLIGHTENMENT is that force which draws Jews
out of their particularism to identifications beyond
the boundaries of Judaism, so it is antisemitism which
often acts to keep them within the circle or pushes them
back into it.[1] As we shall see, antisemitism's influence on
individual Jews and on Jewish communities in the modern
world is ambiguous, not clearly predictable in each instance. By devaluing Jews in the eyes of non-Jews—and
hence some Jews also in their own eyes—antisemitism
may produce mild or severe negations of self. Or it may
have entirely the opposite effect, resulting in renewed affirmation of Jewish identity. Thus antisemitism sometimes serves to abet the influence of enlightenment by add-
ing negative reasons for abandoning Jewishness to positive
ones. But it can also act as a counterforce, undermining the
rationalism and universalism upon which enlightenment is
built and inducing a newfound identification with fellow
victims of discrimination or persecution. As we shall see,
antisemitism in given historical situations may work in
both ways at once, weakening Jewish identity for some,
strengthening it for others.

This ambiguity is almost wholly a product of Jewish modernity. Among premodern Jews antisemitism rarely attenuated Jewish identity; it served rather to reinforce it. Antisemitism was believed to be part of the divine plan which God had determined for Israel. Exiled from the Holy Land on account of their sins, Jews expected to suffer at the hands of the gentiles until such time as the messiah would put an end to their travails. The nations of the earth who tormented them were all actors on the stage of that drama, God's agents in dealing with His chosen people.[2] What gentiles thought of the Jews did not really matter; their views were unable to puncture the firm belief that the Jews continued to be the chosen people, theologically at the very center of world history even as it swirled around them, making them the objects rather than the subjects of historical events. The gentiles' perspective on the Jews was, of course, very different. They understood the Jews' suffering as just punishment for their rejection of Christ and expected that it would end only with the Jews' conversion. But a Jew could not share that view, fundamentally opposed to his own, without ceasing entirely to be a Jew. Thus the more Jews were persecuted, the more they clung to their own faith. If necessary, they would die as martyrs in sanctification of God's name.

To be sure, there were exceptional instances. In medieval Spain barriers between Jews and Muslims, later between Jews and Christians, were not as high as elsewhere in Europe. Greek philosophy, mediated through Islam, had influenced a segment of Iberian Jewry to think in universal and rational terms to the point where the particular rituals and even beliefs of Judaism seemed of little consequence.[3] When the situation of Spanish Jewry deteriorated in the late fourteenth century and Jews in various communities were offered the Cross or the sword in 1391, many Spanish Jews chose Christianity. Others converted, without extreme coercion, during the following century. They could, after all, be Aristotelians in Christian garb as well as in Jewish. Some remained secretly Jewish, but even these were ready to pretend they were Christians in order to save their lives. Spanish Jewry thus foreshadows the modern period, a time when identification with non-Jewish values leaves Jewishness—and not just Jews—vulnerable to antisemitism.

It was the European Enlightenment, however, that, as we have seen, inaugurated the identity crisis for modern Jews, as it drew them to new perspectives from which they began to question the content of their Jewishness. Its promise of equality for all humankind extracted the vigor from their belief in their own theological centrality. They could no longer see the nations of the earth as simply tools in the hand of God to chastise His people. But if the gentiles were not mere instruments, then their views mattered. As long as those views bespoke acceptance of the Jews and their integration into society, they did not produce severe identity problems. Judaism might have to stress its universal foundations more to fit in, as Mendelssohn sought to do, and there might be some disagreement about the shape that Judaism would assume in the modern world, but one could grow up as a Jew without a sense of shame about one's origins and affiliation.

From the start, however, acceptance was mingled with rejection, the enticements of enlightenment balanced by the rebuffs of antisemitism. More cruelly, periods of relative tolerance fostered hopes of true equality, weakening particular Jewish identification. But then came renewed rejection just when the armor of self-assurance had been put aside. Charges to which Jews had earlier been invulnerable—Jewish exclusiveness or deviant ethnic characteristics—now cut them to the quick. Once they had begun to share the thinking of non-Jews in matters of science, philosophy, and art, it was not easy for them to declare: "Yet in your prejudice against the Jews you are completely wrong." To varying degrees and in increasing numbers, modern Jews began to agree with the antisemites' image of their own group, with mild or severe consequences for their Jewish identity.

The milder consequences have been so widespread among modern Jews that it is possible to speak of them in general terms without reference to specific individuals or events. Most common has been the division into "good Jews" and "bad Jews." The former are the ones with whom one can identify. They tend to be those least subject to criticism by gentiles. They are clean, soft-spoken, assimilated, hardworking, and scrupulously moral. They contribute to society but do not push themselves forward too much. Reading of their accomplishments in the newspapers instills inordinate pride and pleasure. The bad Jews represent the mirror image and nemesis of the good ones. One is embarrassed by them for one realizes that their behavior is condemned or ridiculed by the majority culture while, unfortunately, they bear one's own name of Jew. Consequently, there is a need to dissociate oneself from them, for they encourage the antisemitism that is bound to strike down the good Jews along with the bad. Hypersensitivity to the actions of the bad Jew is the counterpart of exaggerated satisfaction in the accomplishments of the good.[4]

Antisemitism draws scrutiny also to the self. The Jew who feels rebuffed by gentiles inevitably asks himself: "Was it I who erred by some inappropriate word or act, or was it my Jewishness that gave offense irrespective of what I said or did?" The effect of this uncertainty is a recurrent anxiety that taxes emotional equilibrium.[5] It arouses fears that a false move will provoke the prejudiced judgment: "That indeed is what one would expect from a Jew." The result is strenuous effort to disguise one's Jewish identity, to prevent it from being a calling card.[6] Only after one's virtue has been established, is it permissible to transmit knowledge of one's Jewishness, knowing that, at the very least, the antisemitic gentile will acknowledge you as an exception to his rule about Jews.

A few sample strategies will illustrate the point. Certain family and personal names are decidedly Jewish; they telegraph the Jewish identity of their bearer. Those Jews most concerned with their image in the sight of non-Jews have changed Cohen and Levy to Corbett and Lane, Abraham and Moses to Albert and Morris. When the Austrian prime minister once asked the Jewish deputy from Galicia, Joseph Bloch, whether Archbishop Theodor Cohen of Olmütz had really converted, he replied: "Never fear, your Excellency, if he were still a Jew he would no longer be called Cohen."[7] A similar attempt at disguise is the alteration of prominent physical characteristics that supposedly mark one as Jewish. Erikson relates the case of a psychiatric patient whose prominently Jewish nose made him feel sincerely "that the only true savior for the Jews would be a plastic surgeon."[8] Like the straightening of curly hair among blacks, the "nose job" among Jews serves to reduce the obviousness of minority identity and enable them to believe they removed a symbol that shouts "Jew" before they can present their personal identity for judgment to the gentile. A less extreme way of hiding Jewishness is to overcompensate for gentile prejudice by taking on character traits at the furthest remove from the Jewish stereotype: for example, unbridled generosity, immaculate dress, and impeccable manners. Perhaps the most common and widespread disguise is simply the attempt not to give away Jewish identity too early in a relationship by some obviously Jewish word, gesture, or reference. Thus antisemitic prejudice produces a heightened Jewish self-consciousness in the presence of gentiles, which results in the endeavor to keep Jewishness as invisible as possible for as long as possible to the eye of the untrustworthy outsider whose favor is sought.

Yet this fear of rejection also has a social effect that tends to strengthen Jewish identity. In the desire to escape the anxiety of being a Jew in the social world of gentiles, Jews have preferred to mix socially with one another. Even as the presence of gentiles has made Jews ill at ease, they have felt more comfortable among fellow Jews, where they could relax and not feel they had to be on best behavior.[9] Remarkably, even those modern Jews who gave up official identification with Jews entirely by converting to Christianity often associated almost exclusively with fellow converts. In Germany they were referred to as *Taufjuden,* baptized Jews. They had not really become Christians but taken on a borderline identity in which they still feared the verdict of the born Christian.

In retrospect Jewish embarrassments of this kind seem to have been especially prevalent at times when antisemitism was moderately strong but not so virulent as to make the attempt at gaining acceptance futile. In present-day America both the lower level of social antisemitism and, from the Jewish side, the decreased sensitivity to the opinions of the gentiles following the Holocaust and in the period of the state of Israel have reduced the anxiety.[10] In fact one can detect an opposite reaction in the appearance of large and prominently worn Jewish symbols—especially the Magen David and the *chai*.[11] For many contemporary Jews hiding Jewishness has given way to flaunting it.

38

Antisemitism

In the more densely antisemitic atmosphere of nine-teenth-century Germany widespread contempt for Jews sometimes produced the extreme and pathological phenomenon that has been called Jewish self-hatred.[12] The term has been defined in various ways, either broadly or more narrowly. I wish to use it here in a narrow sense: as a loathing of that in oneself which one deems to be Jewish and wishes to expunge but cannot. It is, to use the language of Lady Macbeth, crying: "Out, damned spot! out, I say!" Yet the spot remains and one feels sullied by it. In the psyche of creative individuals the ineradicable awareness of one's somehow filthy Jewishness can result in a structure of ideas so far removed from reality as to allow of no other explanation than pathology. Two prominent examples will illustrate the point.

However one may judge the validity of Karl Marx's economic and political writings, his early piece on the Jewish question is so eccentric as to beggar rational explanation. Marx was nominally a Christian from the age of six, when his father brought the whole family to the baptismal font. But a grandfather and an uncle were rabbis and there were rabbis on both sides of his genealogy. Marx knew very little about Judaism, but not only was he obviously aware of his origins, he was reminded of them repeatedly by political opponents. In turn, he branded such of his rivals as were Jewish with demeaning epithets like Jüdchen, Jüdel, or Itzig.[13] He remained silent during the pogroms directed against the Jews of Russia in 1881. Later Jewish apologists tried to make Marx a Jew in spite of himself, pointing to his prophetic heritage or messianic striving. But Marx himself never saw his writings as part of any Jewish tradition.[14]

In his 1844 essay entitled "On the Jewish Question"[15] the young Marx drew his definition of Judaism from the

39

antisemitic writer Ludwig Feuerbach. Judaism was not a religion or a peoplehood but the egoistic desire for gain, the love of money. "What is the worldly basis of Judaism? Practical necessity, selfishness. What is the worldly religion of the Jew? Barter. What is his worldly God? Money." The Jew was capitalism incarnate. Marx remained blind to the existence of a Jewish proletariat that was especially numerous in eastern Europe. Incredibly, he equated Jew with bourgeois speculator. But Marx went further. Not alone the historical Jew is a Jew in Marx's new sense. Christians, insofar as they are capitalists, have in essence become Jews. "The practical Jewish spirit has become the practical spirit of the Christian nations." Money is the jealous God of Israel and that God has become the Lord of the universe.[16] Jews are despicable because the bourgeois society that they epitomize is despicable. The emancipation from capitalism (for Marx the bane of modern society) is also the emancipation from Judaism. Marx has projected his own nonacceptance of his Jewish origins upon society as a whole. He need not feel guilty about rejecting the Jewish traditions of his family, for Jewishness is but egoism and avarice. Moreover, being Jewish is not his problem alone. All who participate in capitalist society are more or less Jews. Thus all must trade a wretched Jewish identity for the worldwide fellowship of the proletariat.

Though historically far less significant than Karl Marx, Otto Weininger too was an original thinker whose work was widely read by contemporaries and continues to be the object of academic discussion.[17] Weininger lived out his short life in fin de siècle Austria, the lively capital of sensuality, seedbed of psychoanalysis, and hotbed of antisemitism. He studied philosophy and a variety of sciences at the University of Vienna, where he received his doctorate in 1902. On the same day he converted to Protestant Christianity. In May 1903 Weininger published *Sex and Character,* a work that made him famous. But only four months later he committed suicide, at the age of twenty-three. As far as is known, Weininger's relations with his family were not difficult. His father, who also converted, along with Weininger's sisters, esteemed his son highly. The young Weininger seems not to have had any special problem with things Jewish. Yet he was an intensely troubled person who was driven to define Judaism no less oddly than had Marx.

In *Sex and Character* three influences predominate: Plato, from whom Weininger takes the conception of ideal types; Kant, who gives him the ethic of uncompromising fulfillment of duty; and Christianity, from which he draws the transcendence of nature and the divine soul in man. Weininger's first objective is to create a dichotomy of ideal types of man and woman. The former alone, he argues, possesses logic, ethics, aesthetics; man alone has a soul and a mind. Sexuality is only one part of his make-up. Woman, by contrast, lives only unconsciously and selfishly, lacking all the positive attributes of the man. She is wholly sexual. In philosophical terms, man is form; woman is matter. An actual woman may possess some of the qualities associated with men, but to the extent that she does, she ceases to be a woman.

Judaism too is a Platonic idea. Weininger tells us that it is "neither a race nor a people, even less a recognized creed. I think of it as a spiritual orientation, a psychological constitution which is a *possibility* for *all* mankind, but which has merely become actual in the most conspicuous fashion among the Jews."[18] Judaism is saturated with femininity. Like the woman, the Jew is amoral, capable of neither great goodness nor great evil. He is much absorbed in sexual matters, especially matchmaking, which is the special province of women. Because the Jew, like the woman, lacks a soul, he is beguiled by such soulless doctrines as materialism, Darwinism, and Spinozistic determinism. The present age, Weininger informs his readers, suffers from the linked maladies of femininity and Judaism. Both must be overcome for the sake of humanity. By sustained moral effort the individual Jew can vanquish his amoral Judaism. In practice that means becoming a Christian, for Christ is the great exemplar of the Jew who transcended his Jewishness. By a similar effort individual women can overcome their femininity. They must cease allowing men to use them as sexual objects. Only then, in their chastity, can they, as it were, become men.

Weininger was sufficiently insightful to recognize that he was projecting outward the very qualities that he hated—and feared—in himself. "Whoever detests the Jewish character," he wrote, "detests it first of all in himself. That he persecutes it in others is merely his attempt to separate himself in this way from what is Jewish. He strives to sever himself from it by locating it in his fellow creatures, and so for a moment be able to imagine himself free of it. Hatred, like love, is a projected phenomenon: you hate that person who you feel reminds you unpleasantly of yourself."[19] Of course projection is exactly what Weininger engaged in. Beset by a troublesome awareness of his Jewish origins and irrational guilt over his sensuality,[20] Weininger linked Judaism and sexuality as the bane of modern society, from which it must liberate itself for its own moral welfare. Thus Weininger was able temporarily to divest the private inner struggle of its painful effect by removing it to the public sphere.

The parallel between Marx and Weininger should now be wholly apparent. Each created a mythical Judaism closely linked to those qualities of character from which he was trying desperately to escape: egoism in the one case, lust in the other. Neither man succeeded. Even today Marx continues to be thought of as a Jew, in a sense other than the one he defined, while Weininger has become the parade example of Jewish self-hatred.

Pathological self-hatred, however, is as rare a phenomenon as the Jewish embarrassments discussed earlier are common. To see more clearly the ambiguities of antisemitism's influence on Jewish identity it is necessary to look for those points in history when it appears unexpectedly and to test its effects in relation to its varying degrees of virulence.

The European Enlightenment, as we have seen, played a crucial role in shaping modern Jewish identity since its affirmation of rationalism and universalism enticed Jews to extend identifications beyond the Jewish sphere. In practice, however, the Enlightenment fell short of its ideals. Or to put it differently, its exponents were rarely able to rid themselves fully of the prejudices that ran counter to its spirit. This reality was sometimes difficult for enlightened Jews to accept. Their hopes had been so aroused by the new principles of tolerance that renewed rejections were all the more painful.[21] Some of the Sephardi Jews had begun to greatly admire the grandest spirit of the French Enlightenment, the irrepressible Voltaire. Isaac de Pinto, a prominent Sephardi Jew of French origin, who lived mostly in Holland, wrote that he considered himself Voltaire's greatest admirer and doubted that anyone had read his works more diligently. But however much Voltaire might cherish the ideal of a common humanity, he had displayed little love of the Jews as individuals. He declared them an "ignorant and barbarous people who have long united the most sordid avarice with the most detestable superstition and the most invincible hatred for every people by whom they are tolerated and enriched."[22] Voltaire's attack especially stung those Jews who cherished his writings. Like so many verbal assaults that would follow during the modern period, it had a twofold effect. On the one hand it drew Jews together in defense; on the other it split their ranks.

Isaac de Pinto undertook to write an apology for all of his coreligionists, Sephardim and Ashkenazim alike. He exculpated the Ashkenazim for whatever faults they might possess by attributing their shortcomings to the antisemitism they had suffered. "The contempt that is heaped on them," he wrote, "stifles every seed of virtue and honor." But his main concern was to deflect Voltaire's critique from the circle of closer identification, his fellow Sephardim. Voltaire should have begun his article in the *Philosophical Dictionary* by distinguishing the Spanish and Portuguese Jews from "the common herd of Jacob's other descendants." He tells Voltaire that a Sephardi Jew of Bordeaux and a German Jew of Metz are "two totally different beings." Their manners and values differ radically. If Sephardi Jews have faults, these too are of a different order and rather similar to those of the French upper class. He lists, among others, ostentation, vanity, a passion for women, contempt for physical labor, and supercilious pride. But these, he notes, are the "vices of noble spirits."[23] Though he tries to excuse the Ashkenazi Jews, to some extent Pinto shares Voltaire's contempt for them. He does not want to be tarred with the same brush that blackens them. His feelings were shared by fellow Spanish and Portuguese Jews. When emancipation for the Jews of France became an issue toward the end of the eighteenth century, the French Sephardim sought to block immediate political equality for their Ashkenazi brethren. Although differences between Sephardim and Ashkenazim had been of long standing, the hostility of Voltaire and of others with similar views drove them further apart.

Another incident in the eighteenth century produced a very different effect. In his desire to gain acceptance among non-Jews, Moses Mendelssohn had studiously avoided entering into religious polemics with gentiles. Apparently he believed that the enlightened non-Jewish world would accept his Jewishness as a private matter and judge him on his human qualities and talents alone. Mendelssohn's response in the well-known incident where the Swiss pastor Johann Caspar Lavater called on him either to convert to Christianity or to defend his faith illustrates a very different effect of intolerance. Here Lavater's challenge led not to any dissociation from Judaism or fellow Jews but to a turning point in Mendelssohn's career. He now became a defender of Judaism in the public arena, creating an ideology that justified the persistence of Jewish identity in an enlightened world. Here disappointment with the views of a Christian clergyman, who thought himself tolerant, ironically brought Jewish commitment to the surface in Mendelssohn himself and indirectly worked to sustain it in others as well.

During the nineteenth century antisemitism in Europe continued in two forms. Consistently it remained beneath the surface in the form of varying degrees of official or unofficial discrimination, to a greater extent in eastern than in western Europe. And from time to time it drew major attention to itself through an incident, legal setback, or outbreak of violence. In both forms it played an ambiguous role. Among those Jews whom enlightenment had drawn furthest from Judaism, the knowledge that their Jewishness would always be a hindrance to their careers and a continuing source of anxiety in the presence of gentiles induced efforts to shield or disguise their identity as best they could and in extreme instances to flee from it through conversion. But ongoing discrimination also kept most Russian Jews within their Pale of Settlement and for long out of contact with European culture; and it closed gentile social circles to Jews in the West. Thus it tended to reinforce Jewish identifications for large numbers. As it had in premodern times, antisemitism in the nineteenth and early twentieth centuries continued to shore up Jewish identity by creating external barriers to assimilation.

However, the specific influence of antisemitism on Jewish identity in this period can best be evaluated by examining those occasions when it gains in prominence, calling particular attention to itself and requiring Jews to acknowledge and deal with its renewed virulence. For the Jews of Germany the first such occasion arose during the period of political reaction following the final defeat of Napoleon in 1815. Having served in the Wars of Liberation against the French, they expected confirmation of their emancipation but encountered instead new restrictions, anti-Jewish propaganda, and in 1819 outbreaks of violence. It was a turn of events that stung them to the quick. Their Jewish shell punctured by the force of enlightenment, they were far more vulnerable to enmity than previous generations had been. In Berlin, conversions, which had begun to rise sharply at the beginning of the century, now reached unprecedented heights.[24] For these men and women Judaism was not sufficiently valued to be worth the sacrifice of a coveted career or even social exclusion. For others, the response was to reshape Jews and Judaism by planing away the ragged edges that offended gentile eyes. They spoke of regeneration and reform, cited universalistic passages from Jewish texts, and

46

argued that Judaism was a faith that avowed loyalty to the state in which Jews lived. They tried to show that they could relate to their tradition with the academic detachment and scientific scholarship that prevailed in the universities. All of these responses were, of course, partly prompted by the internalization of just those values that their opponents accused them of lacking. But the renewed atmosphere of rejection lent an urgency to their striving that sometimes robbed it of dignity. Resurgent antisemitism did not allow the process of modernization to run its natural course. Not what was best for the Jews and Judaism but what would diminish antisemitism often became the dominant consideration. And yet the forms of Jewish identity that emerged in Germany during the 1820s and 1830s, the period when the hope of complete equality dimmed the most, proved viable for German and non-German Jews alike: the various types of modern Jewish religiosity, ranging from Neo-Orthodox to Reform, and the *Wissenschaft des Judentums* (the scientific study of Judaism), which created a more reliable version of the Jewish past from which to draw the historical component of Jewish identity.

In the decade before and the decade after midcentury, two antisemitic incidents called forth remarkable and unprecedented international Jewish reactions. In 1840 the Jews of Damascus were accused of ritual murder and stood at risk of mass execution. It was but one more example in a long chain of such accusations, but the first major one in modern times, and it served to reawaken a dormant sense of worldwide Jewish unity and mutual responsibility.[25] It prompted Jews in various lands to unite in an effort to avert disaster. As far away as the United States they held protest meetings. Two outstanding Jewish notables, Moses Montefiore of England and Adolphe

47

Crémieux of France, traveled to the Middle East in a successful attempt to intercede for their fellow Jews.

Even more significant in strengthening Jewish consciousness was the Mortara Affair of 1858. When a Jewish child of the Mortara family living in Bologna, Italy, who had been secretly baptized by a Christian domestic servant was abducted to a monastery, the case produced a shocked reaction among gentiles and Jews. As in the Damascus Affair, Jews were aroused to united efforts—this time in vain—to intercede with various authorities. But now there were longer lasting results. The Mortara Affair was directly responsible for the formation of two Jewish organizations whose task it would be to protect Jewish rights. In 1859 twenty-four American congregations joined to create the Board of Delegates of American Israelites, which numbered among its purposes the defense of Jewish civil and religious rights in the United States and abroad. In an American Jewish community hitherto fiercely divided into religious and ethnic factions, the Board of Delegates soon brought most of them together in a common cause. It was the first American Jewish organization to enjoy such widespread support.[26] Likewise in the wake of the Mortara Affair, French Jewry in 1860 created the Alliance Israélite Universelle, an international organization intended to combat antisemitism everywhere in the world and to aid those Jews who suffered its consequences. Both organizations served to foster a sense of Jewish solidarity during a period when such loyalties had ebbed in the wake of national allegiances.

The Damascus and Mortara affairs, however, did not appear as major setbacks for Jewish emancipation. The former had occurred in the backward Near East; the latter was only a single incident. It was not until the last decades of the nineteenth century that dramatic reversals in the

Antisemitism

status and situation of European Jewry occurred in both East and West. In eastern Europe an outbreak of pogroms and the restrictive May Laws, which both followed upon the assassination of the relatively liberal Tsar Alexander II in 1881, were like a hammer blow that scattered sparks in all directions. Masses emigrated to North America. Usually leaving their traditional religious practice behind, they developed new Jewish identities harmonizable with American democracy. Others remained secure in the shelter of a traditional Judaism, which the brief and limited enlightenment in Russia had penetrated for only a relative few. Smaller numbers turned away to revolutionary socialism or combined socialism with some degree of Jewish ethnic identity. And a few became Zionists. Thus in Russia new enmity hastened dispersion and the multiplication of identity-defining Jewish ideologies.

In Germany and Austria the legally secured and complete political emancipation gained in the late 1860s came under attack little more than a decade later. By the 1880s and 1890s the liberal tide of the preceding two decades had reversed itself and German-speaking Jews once again, as in the years following 1815, felt renewed pressure. This time they were in some respects less vulnerable, in others more so. Over the course of half a century they had learned to adapt to their peculiar status. Their religious ideologies were now less open to charges of exclusivism; their religious practices more occidental in form. Judaism had proved its capacity to adjust to and survive in modern Europe. But for much larger numbers than in 1815 Jewish identity had worn away at the center and become peripheral. Once again—and this time in larger numbers given the increase in Jewish population—the most estranged bowed to the pressure and converted. In Vienna the rate was especially high.[27]

Other Jews, as alienated from Judaism as the converts, refrained from following the same path; they thought it dishonorable to let sheer opportunism motivate the exchange of one religious identity for another. They despised the converts less for having abandoned anything valuable than for giving in to bigotry. Their own essentially contentless Jewish identity became known as *Trotzjudentum*, a Judaism of defiance or spite. It consisted of stubborn refusal to let antisemitism determine their actions.

The new antisemitism also operated as a divisive force. It inclined German Jews to find scapegoats. The most obvious candidates, of course, were the *Ostjuden*, the recent immigrants from eastern Europe, who were the least assimilated in speech and conduct. Repeatedly German Jews blamed the *Ostjuden* for spoiling their carefully cultivated image and distanced themselves from the newcomers, just as the Sephardim had from the Ashkenazim a century earlier. Other voices accused opposing religious factions. The Orthodox Jewish press blamed the Reform or Liberal Jews for bringing down God's wrath in the form of the new antisemitism while Liberal Jews claimed it was all the fault of the Orthodox for remaining too visibly different. Jewish writers of various backgrounds admitted that what the most prominent antisemites said about the Jews had *some* truth with regard to *some* Jews. In replying to antisemitic writers, they bent over backward to meet them halfway. In agreeing that Jews still required "improvement," they succumbed to the judgment of their opponents.

However, both in the short term and the long, the resurgence of antisemitism in Germany also worked to shore up Jewish identity. Even individuals who were least assertive in their Jewishness were driven to take sides, raising their level of Jewish awareness. Indifferent Jews became, as one writer said, "Jews by the grace of [the antisemite Adolf] Stoecker."[28] Remarkably, the antisemitism of 1880 even prompted a small Jewish revival. That year, for instance, Jewish banking houses in Berlin took the unprecedented step of sending out a circular informing all their customers they would be closed on the two days of the New Year and the Day of Atonement. A Jewish newspaper claimed that the agitation had notably increased the extent of Jewish identification, and more than one rabbi regarded this positive effect of antisemitism as nothing less than providential.[29]

The longer term results were more significant. When antisemitism persisted, the German Jews in 1893 finally created a national organization whose chief purpose would be defending the Jews against their enemies.[30] The Central Association of German Citizens of the Jewish Faith soon became, and remained until Nazi times, the largest organization of German Jews. While it continued to invest its energies principally in the defense of Jewish rights, the organization increasingly fostered both Jewish pride and a broader and deeper Jewish identity. Although the association became the sworn enemy of the Zionists, it persistently condemned apostasy and preached the open acknowledgment of Jewishness before gentiles. One association lecturer was able to picture the work of defense not only as heroic but also as linked, however tenuously, to the Jewish past. "Just as our ancestors went boldly and undaunted into exile and death on account of their religion," he maintained, "so let it be said of us some day that we fought fearlessly and tenaciously for our rights."[31] For many religiously indifferent Jews—in Germany, Austria, the United States, and elsewhere—defending their right to be treated equally while remaining in some, even minor, way different from gentiles became their way of being Jewish.[32]

The Dreyfus Affair presents a last example of Jewish response to nineteenth-century antisemitism. French Jewry had quietly adapted to the ways of its fatherland, encouraged by the equality granted it during the French Revolution and pressured by the heavy-handed demands for integration imposed by Napoleon. When antisemitism appeared in the 1880s, Jewish identity in France rested on a fragile base of ethnic descent. The charges of treason made against Captain Alfred Dreyfus in 1894 cast aspersions on the loyalty of French Jews. With few exceptions, Jewish newspapers, organizations, and individuals responded by simply reaffirming allegiance to France or minimizing the apparent change in atmosphere.[33] Unlike their German coreligionists, the Jews of France emerged from their ordeal without any new determination to stand united as Jews against domestic antisemitism. The Dreyfus Affair seems only to have added impetus to the ongoing process of Jewish assimilation in France.

In Germany the ambiguous impact of antisemitism on Jewish identity came to an end during the 1930s. Nazism differed from previous antisemitisms in closing off the escape route of greater assimilation or even conversion. Since the Nazi criteria for Jewishness were essentially racial, converts to Christianity of Jewish parentage were subjected to the same discrimination as the most orthodox Jews. The state now forced Jewish identity on those whom it defined as Jews regardless of their own feelings. No matter what they did—unless they could manage to leave Germany or chose to commit suicide—German Jews were unable to remove themselves from the reference

Antisemitism

group to which they were assigned. They could subjec-
tively reject their externally imposed identity and continue
to maintain that to varying degrees they were ex-Jews, but
to do so meant to create an untenable rift between the way
Jews were treated, formally and informally, on the one
hand and their own self-conception on the other. Even the
disguise of obvious Jewishness through a gentile name was
blocked when the Nazis insisted that every male Jew add
the name "Israel," every female the name "Sarah." Few
were the instances of individuals who could maintain a
subjective consciousness of being no longer, or only minimally, a Jew despite the objective mark placed on all
members of the Jewish "race." The more common response was to look inward at a Jewish interior landscape
that had long ago grown barren.

Nazi antisemitism before the Holocaust thus had the
general effect of restoring Jewish consciousness where it
had eroded severely. The most assimilated of German
Jews, often for the first time in their lives, now felt the
need to confront and to reaffirm their Jewishness. At the
age of twenty-four, the Nobel Prize winning Jewish
chemist Fritz Haber had converted to Protestantism for
the sake of his career. As the head of an important scientific institute, he became an influential figure, especially
after he succeeded in developing poison gas for the German army in World War I. But as a racial Jew, Haber was
forced into resigning his position in 1933. Nazism remade
Haber into a Jew in spite of himself. To Albert Einstein he
wrote: "In my whole life I have never been so Jewish as
now."[34]

Max Liebermann, the most important German Jewish
painter, had never converted to Christianity. Nor had he
hidden his Jewishness. He had even devoted some of his
oeuvre to Jewish themes. But Liebermann was foremost a

53

German and a decided opponent of Jewish nationalism.[35] In the early 1920s the Hebrew poet Hayyim Nahman Bialik had sat for a portrait in Liebermann's studio in Berlin all the while seeking to persuade the artist of the virtues of Zionism. Not surprisingly, Bialik's efforts were of no avail. Liebermann believed that the Jewish question had already been solved. But then, a little over a decade later and just after Hitler had come to power early in 1933, there was a fresh contact between the two men. The aged Liebermann wrote to Bialik, then in Palestine, in order to thank him and Meir Dizengoff, two of the curators of the Tel Aviv museum, for that body's decision to name a room in his honor. After expressing his joy at the tribute, Liebermann continued in this little-known letter:

In these difficult times the feeling of solidarity with my Jewish coreligionists is doubly gratifying and comforting in view of the deprivation of rights with which German Jews are now forced to live. Like a horrible nightmare the abrogation of equal rights weighs upon us all, but especially upon those Jews who, like me, had surrendered themselves to the dream of assimilation. You, Herr Bialik, perhaps remember the conversations we had on this subject when I was etching your portrait. Then I sought to explain why I kept my distance from Zionism. Today I think differently. As difficult as it has been for me, I have awakened from the dream that I dreamed my whole life long. Unfortunately, so old a tree—I will be 86 years old next month—is beyond transplanting.[36]

Younger German Jews, who likewise had not been Zionists, did go to Palestine in large numbers during the early Hitler years. Those who remained behind sought to fill their externally reimposed Jewish identity with Jewish content. Synagogues that had stood nearly empty during the Weimar period now filled with Jews who sought them out as refuges from the hostility they encountered in daily

Antisemitism

life.[37] Prayers long forgotten assumed new meaning as Israel, once again, became a people apart. Jewish education experienced a revival as Jewish children were expelled from the general schools or their lives there made odious by the harassments of the Hitler Youth. In Berlin and elsewhere Jewish cultural institutions too became the focus of widespread interest. During its most difficult years German Jewry embarked on a remarkable project to reeducate itself to an ineluctable Jewish identity. Looking back, one writer termed this effort paradoxically "construction on the eve of destruction."[38]

In France, too, during the brief period between Nazi occupation and deportation, there arose a new sense of the common destiny of the Jewish people, which pushed aside long-standing antagonisms between native French and east European Jews.[39] In Poland, Nazi-imposed ghettoization did not expunge the differences among established Jewish parties of differing ideologies. But there, as well, external pressure, now in the form of physical segregation, brought those Jews who had strayed the farthest back into the Jewish fold. At least at first, Jewish life in the teeming ghettos was remarkably vibrant.

Of course, whether in Germany, France, or eastern Europe, the revival of Jewish consciousness was short-lived. The worsening situation undermined morale and drove up the rate of suicides. For many the reaffirmation of their Jewishness came only on the eve of an unwilled martyrdom. If Nazi antisemitism briefly reawakened Jewish identity in some hitherto alienated Jews, its ultimate end was to snuff it out altogether along with the lives of those in whom it dwelt. For the victims, inescapable Jewishness turned into an inescapable fate as Jews.

In succeeding years the recollection of this most extreme instance of antisemitism could not easily create a Jewish

55

identity where none had been fostered in childhood. The European social philosopher Jean Améry emerged from Auschwitz with a number on his arm but a Jewishness that was sustained almost exclusively by fear and anger. "No one can become what he cannot find in his memories," Améry wrote after the war. His Jewishness, imposed by antisemitism, had resulted in an enduring commitment to endangered fellow Jews. But it could not create a Jewish identity. Again in Améry's own words: "The environment in which I had lived in the years when one acquires one's self was not Jewish, and this cannot be reversed. But the fruitlessness of the search for my Jewish self by no means stands as a barrier between me and my solidarity with every threatened Jew in this world."[40]

Yet just as ironically as Nazism had initially given the impulse to a deepened Jewishness so did the Holocaust eventually become a major factor in sustaining Jewish identity after World War II. Jewish leaders in the United States early called for a revitalized American Jewish community that would be capable of compensating in some measure for the loss of east European Jewry. Later, and in particular following the Eichmann trial of 1961, Holocaust awareness increasingly became a major portion of what it meant to be Jewish, especially in the Diaspora. Few American Jews were survivors in the literal sense, but the notion that every Jew living in the post-Holocaust age was a kind of survivor gained increasing acceptance. Whereas before the Shoah American Jewish identity was for most Jews either a religiously based morality or a loose bond of ethnic solidarity, the rise in awareness of the Holocaust produced in many individuals a much more determined Jewishness. They were bent on preventing the identity Hitler sought to expunge through physical destruction from succumbing to the subtler pressures of assimilation. In western Europe greater geographical proximity to the events resulted in a closer focus on the Holocaust and a sense of building upon the ruins of the Jewries that were destroyed. Even in the Soviet Union recollection of the catastrophe became a focal point for Jewish revival beginning in the early 1960s.[41]

In the United States a large share (some have argued too large a share) of Jewish activity has been devoted to keeping alive the memory of the Holocaust and fighting contemporary forms of antisemitism. Most young Jews know more about the Shoah than they do about any other period of Jewish history. Courses on the Holocaust in colleges and universities are far more popular than other offerings in Jewish studies. Scores of Holocaust institutions keep alive the memory through exhibits, conferences, and educational literature. While American Jews continue to think of themselves, at least nominally, as Orthodox, Conservative, Reform, or Reconstructionist, this religious identity does not, for most of them, possess the same salience as does the possibility of new danger to their existence. It is in large measure the memory and message of the Holocaust that create a basis for Jewish unity in spite of religious diversity. Concern for the future of the *Jews* seems to run deeper than concern for the future of the *Jewish religion*.[42]

Antisemitism in the contemporary Jewish Diaspora, and especially in the United States, has thus ceased to be ambiguous in its effect. Neither the memory of the Holocaust nor the relatively low levels of current discrimination are driving Jews to hide their Jewishness, let alone to apostatize. On the contrary, antisemitism, especially as collective memory, serves as a basic motive for Jewish identification. The erosive force today comes almost exclusively from the enlightenment side, from the absence of barriers inhibiting the contact between Jews and non-Jews. Jews do not, as before the Holocaust, marry gentiles to escape the odium of discrimination. If they intermarry—as they continue to do in ever-increasing numbers—it is rather because universal values have displaced particularism in both communities. Thus in their effect on Jewish identity enlightenment and antisemitism have come into direct opposition. Today, antisemitism serves almost exclusively to shore up and intensify Jewish identity.

Zion

❧

The Centripetal Force
of Jewish Peoplehood

IN THE RICH spiritual treasury of the Jewish religion
there is no more powerful symbol than Zion. As Sinai
signifies the coalescence of a loosely formed band of Israelites into a people covenanted with God, Zion represents the fulfillment of that covenant. On Mount Zion in
Jerusalem the people established its worship; thrice yearly
they made pilgrimage to it. When the Romans destroyed
the Second Temple and the Holy Land was lost, Zion
became both a memory of earlier glory and the hope of yet
greater glory to come. As a messianic symbol it came to
represent both the Return of the people to its land and the
Redemption for Israel and all humanity. In no small measure it was the unfulfilled dream of Zion that kept Jews
loyal to their faith.

Jewish enlightenment did not attempt to destroy the
immensely pervasive power of Zion. It only altered its
contours. Reason stripped the concept of miraculous elements; universalism shifted its focus from the particular
redemption of Israel to the reign of peace among all nations. But, insofar as they remained Jewish at all, rationalists and universalists continued to focus their Jewish iden-

tity forward toward the unattained ideal. In the Prophets of ancient Israel Jewish modernists found the vision of a universal Zion whose symbolic center was Jerusalem. It was precisely the messianic task, Jews in the West argued, that made Jewish survival necessary and the escape from Judaism on account of discrimination and persecution into a betrayal of Israel's mission. Antisemitism represented both the world's rejection of the ideal and the Jews' need to suffer for its realization. Thus, even rationalized and universalized in the crucible of modernity, Jewish messianism continued, as in earlier times, to act as a centripetal force, uniting Jews in the common conviction that Zion had not yet been realized. To be a Jew, in addition to all its other meanings, retained the fundamental sense of living in an unredeemed world.

Nonetheless, Zion also served as a symbol of division. Traditional Jews waited for God to send the messiah, who would lead Israel back to its land. They associated Zion with the reinstitution of animal sacrifices in a rebuilt Temple. They believed they could hasten the Redemption only through more scrupulous adherence to the divinely ordained moral and ritual law. But modern religious Jews, dwelling within the context of emancipation, either played down the Return to Zion, assigning it to a distant time and depriving it of any immediate political consequences (as did modern Orthodoxy), or gave up the hope of Return entirely and removed it from the liturgy (as did Reform). Jewish socialists substituted a messianic vision of their own in which all of suffering humanity, not Israel in particular, was deemed needful of worldly redemption.

The modern Zionist movement rejected both the older relationship to Zion and its recent reinterpretation. Zionism valued traditional Jews' unwillingness to exchange the tangible Zion of the land of Israel for a universalized ideal.

Zion

And it even sought to recapture something of the undiluted particularism of the as yet unmodernized Jews in eastern Europe. But it could not accept the ingrained, divinely sanctioned passivity predicated on the belief that Redemption was not to be wrought by human hands. For a Jew to become a Zionist was to assume personal responsibility for the people's destiny.

Zionism's relation to enlightenment was similar. As Zionism would not have been possible without the millennial hope of Return nurtured by Judaism through the ages, so it required the heritage of enlightenment precisely in order to transcend the passivity of tradition. It was secular analysis that brought Zionists to reject the view that exile and antisemitism were God's punishment for Israel's ancient sins. It was faith in the operation of reason in the world that prompted political Zionists to lay out their ambitious plans. But enlightenment had led to an assimilation that young Zionists in the West knew intimately from their own families. Jewish universalism was eroding the capacity for Jewish survival. And enlightened Jews had manifested a poor capacity to resist the debilitating impact of antisemitism. They had allowed it to minimize their Jewishness out of fear of giving offense. The need ever and again to prove adherence to the political structures and national values of the states in which they lived had forced Westernized Jews to squeeze Jewish identity into the narrow confines of religious affiliation. To become a Zionist, therefore, was to transcend the pernicious effects of enlightenment and antisemitism even while utilizing their benefits. Henceforth reason would serve national purposes; antisemitism would not only act as a brake on assimilation, its unhappy consequences would point to Zionism as the only adequate solution to the ubiquitous "Jewish Question." Zionism, then, set out to redirect old

61

and new forces operating upon Jewish identity from within and from without, using their energy to forge a new movement.

Where the movement's supporters differed greatly among themselves was on the precise nature of Zionist identity.[1] Closest to tradition were the religious Zionists, for whom Zionism was a natural outgrowth of Judaism. They favored settlement of the land and could view the Zionist enterprise as the beginning stages of the promised Redemption, but they insisted that its final consummation remained in the hands of God. For them Zionism was not a substitute for the older form of Jewish identity. They saw themselves as still fundamentally Jews in the pre-Zionist sense, except that they were willing to join secularists in a common enterprise. In an ultimate sense, Zion continued to mean for them the rebuilding of the Temple and the establishment of a society governed fully by Jewish law. Their Zionism was conditional upon the movement's maintaining neutrality on questions of religion and culture.

Religious adherents allied themselves most closely with the political Zionists, whose most prominent spokesman was Theodor Herzl, the founder of the international Zionist movement. There was a lack of ultimacy in Herzl's vision that made it easier for those traditional Jews drawn to Zionism to cooperate with him. Political Zionists were generally willing to hold questions of Jewish content in abeyance. Their principal concern was to rescue Jews from the physical and spiritual effects of antisemitism. The Jewish society in the land of Israel that Herzl envisaged would approximate the more enlightened societies of Europe. Within that society the Jewish religion would have a role not greatly different from what it was in the Diaspora.

Zion

Herzl attempted neither to secularize Judaism nor to absorb religion within national culture. Although political Zionism, with its insistence that antisemitism was a permanent feature of Jewish life in the Diaspora, challenged Western Jews' sense of security, it was not directed against any particular forms of Jewish expression. It did not berate the religious positions of either modern Orthodoxy or Reform Judaism in the West; it did not criticize traditional values still cherished in the East. Minimally, one could become a political Zionist simply out of the conviction that Jews in distress required a safe refuge—somewhere in the world. As the Zionism of Louis Brandeis in the United States attests, such philanthropic sentiments and the activities flowing from them did not necessarily require a reorientation of personal loyalties or values. For other Jews in the West, especially those without firm religious faith, political Zionism did provide a new, national identity, but only very rarely did it motivate any radical change in the pattern of their lives.[2]

For existing forms of Jewish identity it was cultural Zionism that offered the most serious challenge. Ahad Ha-Am, its progenitor and chief spokesman, was an agnostic in belief, a non-halakhic Jew in practice. For him, unlike for Herzl, Zionism was not principally a matter of externals. It was less a question of altering the conditions under which Jews lived than of transforming the Jews themselves. Herzl's goal was to give Jews like himself—Europeans of the Jewish religious denomination—their own state, where they could live at peace, freed from the scourge of antisemitism. Ahad Ha-Am wanted to transform the Jews' inner Jewish self. Religion would cease to be its indispensable essence.

Yet from the very beginning of Jewish history, belief in the God of Israel had been a sine qua non of what it meant to be a Jew. Until modern times there was no intermediate position between faith in the God who revealed His will to the Jews and conversion to some other religion. Still in the nineteenth century Jews in western and central Europe—no matter how much they assimilated culturally, no matter how little time they spent in the synagogue—as long as they remained Jews, they did not openly assault the religious foundations of Jewish identity. Even when Jews in the West possessed little personal faith, they defined their Jewishness in religious terms, for that was the mode of differentiation allowed them in societies that possessed little tolerance for a pluralism of cultures. Enlightened Jews in eastern Europe possessed somewhat more understanding for a Jewish identity divested of religious belief and practice. But as the more radical of the maskilim became secularists, they moved rapidly beyond Jewish identity elements of any kind. They severed their ties with Judaism, considering themselves only of Jewish origin, while identifying positively as members of a universal proletariat or an enlightened humanity. Even the use of Hebrew among them gave way before the Russian language. Although Jewish socialists, members of the Bund (the Marxist General Union of Jewish Workers), held on to Yiddish as the secular language of the Jewish proletariat, they used it only as an instrument to reach the masses in the Pale of Settlement. Secularism seemed ineluctably to lead out of Judaism.

Ahad Ha-Am, the east European Jewish intellectual, sought to reverse this trend by creating a Zionism that would draw secularists back into the Jewish orbit, not merely as proponents of a political project but as bearers of a pervasive Jewish identity. His task was to show that being a secular Jew was not wholly discontinuous with a Jewish past dominated by religion. He therefore cast his eyes on those elements in Jewish history with which even philosophical positivists like himself could still identify. Prophetic morality, the Pharisaic balance of body and intellect—these, he argued, were values still deserving of identification. Moreover, they would set the Jews apart in the future as they had in the past.

Ahad Ha-Am's thinking reflects an important shift in the nature of Jewish identity. Jewishness, to his mind, was not adherence to a set of beliefs and practices. Rather it meant possessing a share in the spirit that had created them. The Jewish spirit that animated the people in every age had produced the Jewish religion, but it was also responsible for the Jews' broader intellectual and cultural attainments. Religion was historically its most important component, but it was not its essence. Not surprisingly, Ahad Ha-Am's spiritual, or cultural, Zionism became the bête noire of religious Jews of all kinds, East and West.[3] Whether Orthodox or Reformers, whether for religious reasons or political ones, they were determined to reject a Jewish identity that embraced secularity as Jewishly not less legitimate than religious faith.

For Ahad Ha-Am, Zion represented the goal of the Jewish spirit. To return to Zion was both to return to the physical land of Israel and to create there a new efflorescence of Jewish culture. As the Jewish people could not survive except in continuity with Jewish history, so they could not sustain intense intellectual and cultural productivity apart from the land that had nourished their spirit in ancient times. Other Jewish nationalists disagreed. Simon Dubnow, the historian of the Jews, was no less convinced than Ahad Ha-Am that secular Jewish identity required grounding in the Jewish past, and therefore he sought in his historical work to elaborate how the collective spirit of the Jews had created communal institutions whose fundamental nature and function were veiled by the need to incorporate them "gradually and artificially into the sphere of religion."[4] But, unlike Ahad Ha-Am, Dubnow held that the Jewish spirit could flourish even outside the land of Israel. His form of national Jewish identity was in a sense the purer one. It could be sustained by the will of the people within culturally autonomous Jewish communities anywhere. Jewish creativity required only the landscape of Jewish memory, not the physical land of Israel.[5]

Ahad Ha-Am and Dubnow alike deplored the narrow confines into which recent rabbinic Judaism had driven the Jewish spirit. Conversely, they were confident that, given an inner revival, that spirit could once more expand to a breadth it had attained in earlier periods of Jewish history. Both men intended that wide-ranging intellectual creativity would characterize Jewish culture in the future. But other Jewish nationalists thought they were not going far enough. They found that Ahad Ha-Am, despite his secularism, was, on account of his intellectualism and strong moralism, still too much a Jew of the old type. He was not willing to accommodate within Jewish culture any values—such as those espoused by Nietzsche—that he regarded as wholly alien to the moral orientation of Judaism.[6] More revolutionary ideologists wanted not merely to make room for secularism within a national Jewish identity, they insisted upon the freedom to import doctrines that stood in stark opposition to Jewish tradition, even when that tradition was broadly interpreted. Jewish intellectualism, along with sworn opposition to the delights of the senses, was to their minds as unacceptable a form of identity as was Orthodox religion.

The notion that the character qualities of the Jews would have to change—and not simply their ideology—is present from the very beginnings of the Zionist movement. As

Zion

early as 1882 Leon Pinsker had complained bitterly of the deleterious effects of antisemitism on the Jewish character. It had robbed the Jews of their self-respect, their human dignity, and their national will. The restoration of Jewish nationhood therefore required a psychological transformation that Pinsker called "auto-emancipation." Only after the Jews themselves had changed could they hope to transform their condition in the world. Later Zionists dwelt upon what qualities the Diaspora Jew required in order to gain the capacity for nation-building. Max Nordau, one of Herzl's closest associates, was not only an atheist but, unlike Ahad Ha-Am, a nonbeliever in the importance of historical continuity. "If the Jews are touched by a desire to establish a new kingdom of Zion," he wrote, "their inspiration comes from neither the Torah nor the Mishnah, but from the hardships of the times."[7] What the Jews needed to develop, Nordau argued, was not so much their brains as their muscles. Zionism demanded a new physical Jew, not simply a broadening and secularization of the Jewish spirit. In the long run, only that new Jew, the Zionist, could preserve the Jewish people.[8]

Micha Josef Berdyczewski, the prominent Hebrew writer, was similarly in revolt against excessive Jewish intellectualism. The narrow concentration on spirit, he believed, had led to neglect of the sensual, earthly life. However, unlike Nordau and like Ahad Ha-Am, he recognized the importance of historical precedent in sustaining a collective identity. He therefore drew into consciousness those periods and events of the Jewish past that lent support to a very different self-conception. Especially attractive to Berdyczewski and those who followed in his footsteps were the Maccabees, the ancient warriors for national independence. In Zionist circles the celebration of Hanukah soon came to focus on Jewish heroism rather than the miraculous cruse of oil that lasted for eight days. Zionists also rehabilitated Simeon Bar-Kokhba, the failed military messiah of the second century. To dramatize their new identity they often spoke of themselves as Hebrews rather than Jews.

Some Zionists found historical continuity more in forms than in content. According to Eliezer Ben-Yehuda, the principal reviver of spoken Hebrew, using the language of one's Jewish ancestors could provide a substitute for tradition. The old words could clothe new ideas and make them less foreign. Nahum Sokolow expressed the extreme importance of Hebrew most emphatically when he wrote: "The Hebrew language is our national possession. Every Hebrew word is an echo of the entire nation; every Hebrew word restores to us our past, vivifies our present, and instills trust in our future."[9] In addition to the ancient language, Zionists could root their identity in the land, with the memories it evoked of periods of national independence. Its sunny fields, in which hardy pioneers would till the soil, presented a Zionist counterimage to the ghetto yeshiva, where pale students labored over brittle texts. The Jewish imbalance between history and nature would be set aright. In the endeavor to heal the rift created by lack of continuity, a few Zionists went beyond the external criteria of land and language to the concept of race. The new Jew—or the post-Jewish Zionist—might have little in common with most Jews of his own and preceding generations, but ties of blood connected him with them. They provided a biological bond underlying the diversity of worldview. As one Zionist, Joshua Thon, wrote in 1912: "The unity of the Jews lies in their peoplehood and their race; the twelve million Jews scattered to the ends of the earth are indeed a people on account of the blood that flows in their veins." That race would soon produce a new, intellectually and morally superior human being, whom Thon described as "an exalted human type that would be self-determined, acting through his clear intellect, his inner strength, and feelings suffused with mercy and love."[10]

A most relevant point of inner controversy within the Zionist movement was the question of normalcy. Modern Judaism in the West had made a virtue of the abnormality of Diaspora Jewish existence. Its sense of mission and messianic striving was based on the uniqueness of Judaism and of Jewish existence scattered among the nations. Some Zionists drew the chosenness of Israel into Zionist thinking. The new society they intended to create in the land of Israel would be a more powerful "light unto the gentiles" than the Diaspora Jewish communities, which were necessarily unable to establish a complete model society on their own. Thus Zionism bore within it not only the messianic element of Return but also something of the more universal aspirations that were the product of enlightenment influence. However, the Zionist movement also contained within it ideologists of normalcy, who wanted to create a state and society no different from those of other nations. Insofar as Zionism espoused normalcy, it set itself against all forms of Jewish identity in the Diaspora and provided a parallel in national form to the individual aspirations of Jewish assimilationists, who likewise sought to minimize Jewish differences.

Thus the Zionist movement not only differentiated itself from the bulk of Diaspora Jewry, which long opposed it, but on numerous issues was internally divided as well. Its identity ideal lay in the future; the national Jew, in fact, did not yet fully exist. Some Zionists even admitted that the Jews collectively had still to regain their peoplehood. "We are not yet a people; we are only [individual] Jews,"

lamented Ahad Ha-Am, echoing Pinsker, in 1892.[11]
However much the Zionist movement stressed the national ties binding Jews to each other, it could not set
before world Jewry a consistent image of the new Zionist
Jew. Would he or she be secular or religious, a believer in
Jewish normalcy or chosenness, culturally a European living in a Jewish state or, contrariwise, a Jew by culture,
drawing upon the Jewish spirit to create a focal point of
Jewish particularity in the ancient land? Thus, ironically,
the movement that set out to unify the Jewish people
sowed its share of discord instead. Yet as the ideal of political Zionism neared realization in the wake of Nazism
and the Holocaust, most external Jewish opposition
melted away. Once it became clear that antisemitism was
not a vestige of the past, sympathy with efforts to establish
a refuge for persecuted Jews became an integral part of
Jewishness. As for the nature of Zionism, seen from a
different perspective the variety of positions appeared a
point of strength. Jews of varying political, religious, and
cultural orientations could find a wing of Zionism that
corresponded to their views. Thus, by 1948 Zionism had
fully mobilized the centripetal force of Jewish peoplehood.
With the establishment of the state, its focal significance
for Jewish identity was no longer in question.

Y et the state of Israel itself soon created new and unprecedented questions of Jewish identity. Its very
name presented a problem. *Israel* was the designation by
which God had addressed the entire people. All Jews were
Israel. But henceforth only those who were citizens of the
new state could claim the term fully. Traditional expres-
sions, like "rabbi in Israel," now required further explanation. It became necessary to specify whether one meant
the people or the state. The term *Israeli* was equivocal

Zion

from the beginning. In its most precise, legal sense it meant any citizen of the state—"a person who possesses an Israeli identity card," by one definition.[12] Hence it included non-Jews. Yet *Israeli* is not merely a designation of political status. Beyond citizenship, it is also a category of ethnic identity. To be an Israeli, it is generally believed, means to be a Jew residing permanently in the ancestral land.[13] Even those non-Jewish citizens of Israel who most fully identify themselves as Israelis cannot do so in that sense. An Israeli Arab must feel a certain ambivalence about his political identity. "My country, Israel, is at war with my people, the Arabs," one of them has said.[14]

The term *Israeli* has been no less problematic for Israeli Jews. It is the term of identity that separates existence in the homeland from existence in the Diaspora. *Jew* and *Zionist* are identity designations that unite the Jewish people; *Israeli* divides. Not surprisingly, it is this name that is stressed in discussions that differentiate the two Jewries.[15] Jews who make aliyah from the United States continue to be Jews and Zionists, but they also take on the new identity of Israeli. The inner content of that identity consists of an amalgam of values, many of them rooted in early Zionism. In contrast to Diaspora Jews, Israelis believe themselves to be self-reliant, proud, and unafraid. Unacquainted with antisemitism, the born Israeli, the sabra, lacks hypersensitivity to the opinions of strangers. As an Israeli, the sabra's identity is rooted in a short but colorful history of his or her own.

The Zionist identity of Israelis is much less obvious. The vast majority of Jewish Israelis consider themselves Zionists,[16] but they are not quite certain what that means after 1948. Some simply associate it with Israeli patriotism. For them, as Jews living in a Jewish state, Zionism is merely a commitment to continue the land-settlement and nation-building begun by the first pioneers. For others it represents their link with the widely scattered Jewish people outside Israel. One survey, taken during the Yom Kippur War, showed that 96 percent of Israelis feel they are a part of that Jewish people.[17] Their Zionism therefore requires them to be concerned for physically or spiritually oppressed Jewries all over the world and, above all, to encourage their immigration to Israel. Many feel it also implies, conversely, that all Jews have a share in the state of Israel, not the Israelis alone.[18] Zionism further provides a prehistory for the Israeli experience. The Israeli identity is historically rooted in its Zionist predecessor. And by extension, Zionist history reaches back to earlier times, preceding or paralleling Jewish history. It is the history of those periods when Jews lived in their land and of the longing for Zion when they were forced to live in the Diaspora. It is the history of Jewish villages that existed in the land even during medieval times, and of course it is the history of the modern settlement. But it is emphatically not the history of Jewish suffering; it is not the history of the Holocaust. The latter belong to "Jewish history," not to the Zionist-Israeli continuum. Israeli students, especially those in the secular educational system, perceive times of exile and suffering as essentially negative and periods of normality or heroism as the historical source of their own national identity.[19]

Recently, Zionism has taken on a highly controversial meaning. Just as from the beginning of the Zionist movement the most complete commitment to Zion was personal participation in "redemption" of the land by Jewish settlement, so the deepest expression of Zionism today is considered by some to be the extension of that redemption to Judea and Samaria. The settlers on the West Bank, it is believed, are today's Zionists in the fullest sense, more so even than those who continue to settle on hitherto untilled land within the pre-1967 boundaries. It is this concept of contemporary Zionism that is propounded especially in the Israeli religious school system.[20]

The identity *Jew* in Israel is yet more equivocal than either Israeli or Zionist. Israel's Law of Return defines a Jew for purposes of state as "someone born of a Jewish mother or converted to Judaism and who belongs to no other religion."[21] But this compromise definition is wholly acceptable to very few. Orthodox Jews complain of its failure to specify that conversions must be in accordance with Jewish law. Liberals find birth to a Jewish mother an insufficiently broad criterion. And some secular Israelis reject any religious definition of Jewishness on principle. At best, the law provides a modus operandi, certainly not a basis for Jewish identity.

The determination of what Jewishness means for the Israeli requires distinguishing sharply between religious and secular Jews. As repeated studies have shown, it is the religious Israelis who feel the most Jewish, since Jewishness to them represents more than just an ethnic identity. Their fundamental worldview is determined by the Jewish religion. Not surprisingly, they feel close to Jews in the Diaspora, since they share the same religious commitment. Jewishness for secular Israelis, by contrast, evokes ambivalence. Zionism, after all, was a revolt against the Jewishness that the early Zionists criticized so severely both in eastern and western Europe. It was supposed to transcend Jewish passivity on the one hand and the truncated modern religious identity produced by enlightenment on the other. For some secular Israelis, Zionist and then Israeli identity are still seen as post-Jewish. One survey, taken in the midsixties, found that the majority of Israeli students in secular schools felt that being Jewish was of little or no importance in their lives.[22] Close to one-third, if they were to live abroad, would not wish to have been born Jews. As one student put it: "Jewish religion has no meaning for me. In Israel where all are Jews I don't mind also being a Jew. But outside of Israel—why be a Jew?"[23] The nature of Jewish existence outside the state, admitted a former Israeli minister of education, is beyond the perspective of the native-born Israeli.[24] Israeli Jews have had great difficulty identifying with their counterparts in the Diaspora. They have seen them as essentially different from themselves. Remarkably, almost one-third of Israeli parents and students in one survey actually believed that the main cause of antisemitism lies in the characteristics of Diaspora Jews themselves.[25] About 50 percent of students surveyed saw Diaspora Jews as a "different people."[26] The differences have been especially marked for Afro-Asian Jews, who are ethnically the most distant from the largest Diaspora community in the United States.[27]

With regard to their own self-definition, Israeli secularists also have problems with a Jewish identity that is represented by those who seek to expand the influence of religion in public life. They find themselves at one and the same time Jews in an ethnic sense and opponents of Jews in "a more complete sense," whose efforts to Judaize the state on the basis of Jewish law they firmly reject. They can appreciate the value of the Jewish religion in shoring up the sense of peoplehood in the Diaspora, but that task is not required in the state of Israel.[28] Yet at the same time—but apparently in a non-halakhic sense—nearly all Israelis feel that Israel must somehow be a "Jewish state,"[29] and in recent years feelings of Jewish identification have been more closely linked to religion even among Jews on the secular side of the Israeli spectrum.[30]

Zion

It has been widely observed that the Jewish identity of Israelis increases in salience at times when they feel most isolated from other nations. This was evident both in 1967 and in 1973, when it seemed that only the Jewish Diaspora was Israel's wholehearted ally. It may also be that the feeling of vulnerability experienced before the outbreak of the Six-Day War and in the first days of the Yom Kippur conflict served to diminish the sense of Israeli difference from Jewries elsewhere. Jewish existence in Israel now seemed no less beleaguered than it had been through the centuries in the Diaspora. Israelis began to speak of the danger of a second Holocaust. The Six-Day War was significant for Jewish identity in Israel also in a second sense. Even secular Israelis experienced a quasi-religious sense of salvation when fear turned to triumph and holy places, long in Arab hands, became once more accessible to Israeli Jews.[31] The religious-secular dichotomy was temporarily bridged.

Since 1967 there has been a pronounced tendency on the part of both Orthodox and secular Jews in Israel to associate Jewishness with the struggle against the Arabs. As one leader of messianist Orthodoxy put it: "Since I believe in *segulah* [Jewish chosenness], I consider a man undergoing a test of fire on the Golan Heights or in the Sinai a Jew in the fullest sense of the word, even if he has never been exposed to formal Torah education."[32] While most Israeli Jews still set the term *Jew* in opposition to the term *gentile,* an increasing number set it against *Arab* instead.[33] Some nonreligious Sephardi Jews wear a skullcap—the mark of an Orthodox Jew—lest their Mediterranean appearance lead someone to assume they are Arabs.

Increasingly also, Jewishness in Israel has come to mean not only the belief that Israel should be a Jewish state, but insistence upon the sanctity of the land and the consequent unwillingness to compromise possession of any of its parts for the sake of a political goal. The expansion of Israel is deemed to be God's will. To the Israeli mind in general, Judaism is associated with an intense particularism that values the Jews above others. Thus although not all the Orthodox support retention of Judea and Samaria at any price, Jewishness becomes for Israeli liberals to some degree a negative identity on account of its association with messianic politics. Jewishness and liberalism appear to be in conflict; a political liberal in Israel who stresses his Jewishness is a relatively rare phenomenon.

There is still one other sense in which Jewishness is problematic for some Israelis: one can be a Jew either in Israel or in the Diaspora. But one can be an Israeli only in Israel. With statistics to 1989 showing that more Jews leave Israel permanently than migrate there from the Diaspora, concerned Israelis have increasingly stressed the higher virtue of "Israeliness" and emphasized the negative character of Jewishness in the Diaspora. Only exclusive education in the Israeli identity can prevent emigration. No one has put this more strongly than the prominent Israeli writer A. B. Yehoshua. In a newspaper interview he said:

The continuous use of these two concepts [Israeliness and Jewishness] simultaneously already creates in every child the first notion of emigration from Israel. If you are also a Jew, apart from your Israeliness, then anytime—when you feel like it or when you're in trouble—you can join the Jewish life of the Diaspora. Every six-year-old child has already received from his kindergarten teacher the formula for his *yeridah* [emigration]. She can shout all she wants to about love of the land of Israel. But at the same time she is also telling him: "Look what a marvellous people you belong to, a people that survived in the Diaspora for two thousand years and preserved

76

Zion

its full identity." If so, the child says to himself, then I'll go to Los Angeles too and survive there, and I'll even receive a medal from Jewish history.[34]

The old Zionist doctrine of *shelilat ha-golah* (negation of the Diaspora) regained prominence in the wake of demographic forecasts that, until the very recent surge of Jewish immigrants from the Soviet Union, predicted a diminution in the ratio of Jews to Arabs.

Yet praise of Israeliness and derogation of Diaspora Jewishness have not stemmed the tide of emigration. Lack of precise statistical data makes it difficult to determine the exact number of Israelis who have chosen to live permanently in America. Figures range from a low of 100,000 to over half a million.[35] Similarly to previous Jewish immigrations to the United States, once the process has begun, it tends to increase in momentum as more prospective immigrants have family members and neighbors already absorbed in the new society and able to assist them in acclimatizing to the new surroundings. Younger people, having established themselves economically, bring over their parents to join them.

Israeli *yordim*,[36] as they are called, suffer an identity conflict without precedent in modern Jewish history. Indoctrinated in the high value of life in the Jewish homeland, identifying primarily as Israelis, they do not quite know what they are once they no longer live in Israel. Some actually persuade themselves that America represents the values that their land of origin has abandoned and that some day they will bring back to Israel for the sake of its spiritual revival.[37] But more commonly they simply regard their sojourn in the United States as temporary. Even after years abroad, they continue to believe that they will return to Israel. They are only studying in America or engaging in an interesting adventure or building up capital to live more comfortably in Israel.[38]

The *yordim* are left with no appropriate or acceptable identity. Most find themselves psychologically incapable of adopting the label "Diaspora Jew." Instead, they cling tenaciously to the earlier self-designation of Israeli. And yet, as time passes, they are not really Israelis any more either. Or to put it differently, their self-credibility as Israelis melts away further with each succeeding year abroad. To see themselves as Diaspora Jews is particularly difficult for the secularists among them since that represents adoption of an identity they have been taught to reject as religious and, at least partially, as opposed to being an Israeli. To see themselves as Zionists would be truly absurd. Zionists in contemporary America are Jews who give money to Israel but, in most instances, have little direct personal connection with it.

Despite well-intentioned efforts by local Jewish communities, emigrant Israelis have resisted attempts to absorb them within American Jewry. This has been especially true for the secularists, who see the synagogue, so central an institution of Jewish identity in the Diaspora, on the Israeli model—as strictly a place of worship, which a secular Israeli visits either not at all or only casually on the high holy days. The liberal synagogue is wholly strange to nearly all of them. Israel-oriented community institutions are even more problematic than the synagogue. Raising money for Israel is so clearly a mark of Diaspora Judaism that for a *yored* to do so would mean symbolically moving to the other side of the table. Hence Israelis in America speak of having done their share by serving in the Israeli army or insist that when they return they will invest their hard-earned funds directly in the Israeli economy. Even the thought of sending their children to a Jewish school

Zion

raises ambivalence. Fewer Israelis in America than American Jews do so.[39] For a small number, the tensions inherent in this situation have produced a mild form of self-hatred, most frequently manifest in the attribution of negative motives to other *yordim*—from whom the individual sharply differentiates himself.[40]

What remains for emigrants from Israel are memories of the past and anxiety about the future. They come together in America to sing the old songs with which they grew up or to see an Israeli film that reconnects them with the land. But their children rapidly become Americans. In an irony of Jewish history some of them become ashamed of their foreign-sounding Israeli names. One father expressed the dilemma poignantly: "Assuming that I stay on here, what will happen to my son? I won't go to synagogue! At most I'll tell him stories about my home in the country I left and take him to sing the songs we sang in our youth movements. I am an Israeli, I cannot become a Jew."[41]

If the *yordim* in the United States are an embarrassment to themselves, they are so no less to American Jewry. For the notion that Jews should want to leave Israel flies in the face of American Jews' identification with Israel as an ideal of their own identity. It has been frequently pointed out that nothing so unifies Diaspora Jews as their commitment to Israel. It is for them not merely a place where fellow Jews dwell who are in need of their assistance. It is for many at least potentially what Ahad Ha-Am intended it to be: the center of Jewish life, and beyond that the center of gravity for their own Jewishness. In one survey, 83 percent of American Jews responded that if Israel were destroyed, they would feel as if they had suffered one of the greatest personal tragedies of their lives.[42] Even for Soviet Jewry, despite many years of official propaganda against the Jewish state, Israel has served as the beacon for its limited Jewish and Hebraic revival. Avidly reading the daily newspapers for news of Israel, Diaspora Jews all over the world vicariously live through its military victories and take pride in its cultural and scientific achievements; they feel personally grieved by its tragedies and frustrated at consideration of its manifold and intractable problems. They are intent on retaining their special relationship to the state of Israel although that relationship, more than religious difference, marks them off from non-Jews and, especially in recent years, has often been a spur to anti-semitism.

To be sure, Jewish identity in the Diaspora is still to a very high degree conceived in religious terms. Most Jews in the United States who are serious about their Jewishness join a synagogue belonging to one of the four American Jewish denominations. However, only an inner core of such affiliated Jews is religious in more than a peripheral sense. What draws them to the synagogue is largely the desire for ethnic identification, or, in the language of social psychology, to sacralize their identity.[43] They are concerned for Jewish survival and believe that religion is an important vehicle for ensuring it. Aside from the high holy days, they gather in synagogues in large numbers only when a family member or friend celebrates that ritual of Jewish continuity and survival which is the Bar or Bat Mitzvah ceremony. Those assembled rejoice that another link has been forged in the chain.[44] As the Torah scroll is passed from grandparent to parent to child,[45] symbolic testimony to the continuity of Jewish identity is rendered in the midst of the community. A highlight of the ceremony is the traditional blessing that thanks God for having "kept us alive and sustained us and enabled us to reach this day."

Zion

Never in modern times have Jews in the West been more committed to Jewish peoplehood. And most of them see Israel as its chief embodiment. If the United States continues to affirm cultural pluralism, as it has in recent years, then it would seem likely that for American Jewry the ethnic form of Jewish identity (embracing religion to varying degrees) will become even more characteristic. However, two factors militate against that result.

The first is the gap in culture, values, and religion that separates Israeli and Diaspora Jews. For most American and European Jews it is especially difficult to find common ground with the Israelis of Afro-Asian background, who represent an increasing majority of Israel's Jewish population. Already thirty years ago a young American Jew studying in Israel put it succinctly: "Toward Israel, I feel 'we'; toward Israelis, 'they.' "[46] More recently, some (but by no means all) Diaspora Jews have become disenchanted with Israel's policies in the areas of politics and religion. In response to the rightward drift of Israeli governments and the undiminished influence of the Orthodox parties, unsympathetic Diaspora Jews have felt a growing sense of alienation. Surveys taken during the last decade indicate that, except for the Orthodox, American Jewry's attachment to Israel has declined. Especially is this true among Reform Jews and, more generally, in the younger generation.[47] If differences regarding values continue to widen between segments of Israeli and Diaspora Jewries, they may seriously damage the sense of common identity.

The second factor militating against ethnic unity is the phenomenon of "Jews by Choice." Especially in Reform and Conservative congregations in the United States the number of converts to Judaism has reached proportions where their influence is no longer negligible. As has often been pointed out, Jews by Choice tend to understand Jew-

ishness in terms parallel with Christianity. They see themselves as leaving one faith community for the sake of another. Judaism for them is a religion pure and simple.[48]
They have difficulty in internalizing the profound emotional tie that binds Jews to one another. Few see themselves as taking on Jewish peoplehood, in addition to the
Jewish faith.[49] Ironically, Jews by Choice sometimes
marry born Jews whose Jewishness is peripheral and who
may even be trying to escape from it. What their marriage
partners usually do possess, though, is some vestige of
ethnic attachment. The Jew by Choice has as much difficulty understanding that residue as the born Jew does
comprehending many a convert's extraordinary serious-
ness about the Jewish religion.

Thus Jewish peoplehood seems today a more fragile
basis of modern Jewish identity than it was two decades ago, when Jews everywhere basked in the seemingly
miraculous salvation wrought by the Six-Day War. Tensions and differences between Israel and the Diaspora and
the changing nature of Diaspora Jewry are working to
loosen the bonds of solidarity. Still, the sense of peoplehood remains stronger than any other foundation of common Jewishness. Despite differences, Zion has retained its
influence as the most powerful symbol of Jewish unity and
common destiny.

Conclusion

❧

The Present State
of Jewish Identity

JEWISH IDENTITY today continues to lie within the
fields of force represented by enlightenment, antisemitism, and Zion. Only a minute portion of world Jewry
lives in a situation of such complete self-segregation as to
remain impervious to the influences that induce broader
identifications. Nearly all contemporary Jews feel they are
Jews and at the same time something not specifically Jewish as well. For some, Jewishness remains their principal
orientation in life, the center of their being. These are
mostly the serious religious Jews, of whatever specific denomination, who continue to believe in some sense of
Jewish chosenness and special destiny. For others, enlightenment has drawn them almost entirely outside their Jewish identity. Reason and universalism have worn away
their particular loyalty to Jews and Judaism. Some are basically universalists; others have substituted new particularisms for old. Most actively identifying modern Jews,
however, have in one fashion or another absorbed the
influence of enlightenment. They argue that their Jewishness has nothing to fear from new discoveries of science or
widening cultural horizons and that their universal com-

mitments do not interfere with their Jewish ones. To a greater or lesser extent, they have succeeded in neutralizing the erosive influence that enlightenment exercised in the initial stages of modernization.

Although antisemitism has declined since World War II, it continues to play a major role in determining Jewish identity. Even in countries where antisemitism is least severe, like the United States, Jews nonetheless believe they are potentially endangered. Jewish defense organizations flourish and expand their activities. Supporting them serves as a means of Jewish identification in the present as it has in the past. Since Jews in Israel see their protection of Diaspora Jews as a basic component of the relations between them, the presence of discrimination or persecution in the Soviet Union, Ethiopia, or Syria has also served to energize the Israeli sense of ethnic responsibility. Fortunately, the extreme manifestations of reaction to antisemitism are apparently declining, at least in the West. Opportunistic apostasy has diminished greatly as has Jewish self-hate. Antisemitism has become most important for Jewish identity not as a force operative in contemporary society but as the memory of the Holocaust. The intense consciousness of that event is felt as a particular imperative to preserve Jewishness and as a universal task—based on the Jews' having been singled out—to prevent anything resembling a Holocaust in the future.

It is, however, the sense of Jewish peoplehood that represents the strongest component of Jewish identity today. Although, as noted earlier, Jews by Choice tend to understand Jewishness principally as denominational, most religious Jews link Judaism closely to Jewishness. Their synagogue activities are ways of expressing ethnicity. Attending religious services is something Jews do as members of the Jewish people. Because the ties of peoplehood

Conclusion

remain strong, tensions between Diaspora Jews and Israeli Jews will not quickly dissolve their shared sense of solidarity. Although it is possible that deeper dissent from Israeli policies may lead increasing numbers of Diaspora Jews to apathy, the same differences may also serve to create more apparent multiple communities of identification that span the Israel-Diaspora divide. Those Israeli Jews and Diaspora Jews who agree on matters of religion or Israeli political policies would build a sense of moral community based on their common values, either more particularist or more universalist.

Whatever the outcome, whatever forms Jewish identity may take in the near or long term, to be a Jew vigorously in the modern world will continue to mean confronting new external enticements, sorting them out, and seeking to integrate those that do not contradict the fundamental principles of the Jewish tradition. It will also continue to mean coping with hostility in such a way as to prevent it from misshaping Jewishness either through the internalization of negative stereotypes or through allowing memory of persecutions past and fear of persecutions in the future to become the exclusive, cheerless content of Judaism. Mostly, I trust, Jewishness will focus in the future, as in the past, on Zion. For Zion not only represents Jewish origins and Jewish unity. It is also the symbol of that Redemption which orients Jewish identity to its highest goal and gives it intrinsic meaning.

Notes

❧

Introduction: *The Elusive Character of Jewish Identity*

1. Martin Buber, "The Jew in the World," in *Israel and the World* (New York: Schocken Books, 1963), 167–72 (address delivered at the Lehrhaus in Frankfurt am Main in 1934).

2. Sigmund Freud, "On Being of the B'nai B'rith," *Commentary*, March 1946, 23; Erik H. Erikson, *Identity and the Life Cycle* (New York: W. W. Norton, 1980), 109. Erikson prefers to translate *Heimlichkeit* as "secret familiarity"; see his *Childhood and Society* (New York: W. W. Norton, 1950), 241.

3. See especially Philip Gleason, "Identifying Identity: A Semantic History," *Journal of American History* 69 (1983): 910–31. In 1986 Carl N. Degler suggested in his presidential address to the American Historical Association that the presentation of American history should increasingly be shaped around the question, What does it mean to be an American? (*American Historical Review* 92 [1987]: 2). Jürgen Habermas put the problem of collective identity into a universal philosophical and political framework in his "On Social Identity," *Telos* 19 (Spring 1974): 91–103. And various historical studies over the last two decades have explored the complex and uneven emergence of national identities. See, for example, Eugen Weber, *Peasants into Frenchmen: The Modernization of Rural France, 1870–1914* (Stanford, Calif.: Stanford University Press, 1976), and John A. Armstrong, *Nations before Nationalism* (Chapel Hill: University of North Carolina Press, 1982).

4. Erik H. Erikson, *Identity: Youth and Crisis* (New York: W. W. Norton, 1968), 9.

5. Ibid., 159.

6. The term is from Uriel Tal, "Jewish Identity" (in Hebrew), *Ha-Arets,* 12 October 1986, 11.

7. Leon Festinger, *A Theory of Cognitive Dissonance* (Stanford, Calif.: Stanford University Press, 1962).

8. Erikson's language in his *Childhood and Society,* 270.

9. I have here slightly modified the categorization presented by Michael Oppenheim in his "A 'Fieldguide' to the Study of Modern Jewish Identity," *Jewish Social Studies* 46 (1984): 215–30.

10. Much work of this type has been done in recent years by Simon N. Herman. See his *Israelis and Jews: The Continuity of an Identity* (Philadelphia: Jewish Publication Society, 1971) and his *Jewish Identity: A Social Psychological Perspective* (Beverly Hills: Sage Publications, 1977). See also Arnold Dashefsky and Howard M. Shapiro, *Ethnic Identification among American Jews: Socialization and Social Structure* (Lexington, Mass.: Lexington Books, 1974); Arnold Dashefsky, ed., *Ethnic Identity in Society* (Chicago: Rand McNally, 1976); Marshall Sklare and Joseph Greenblum, *Jewish Identity on the Suburban Frontier: A Study of Group Survival in the Open Society,* 2d ed. (Chicago: University of Chicago Press, 1979); and Steven M. Cohen, *American Modernity and Jewish Identity* (New York: Tavistock, 1983). Harold S. Himmelfarb presents a survey of theoretical and field studies relating to American Jewry in his "Research on American Jewish Identity and Identification: Progress, Pitfalls, and Prospects," in Marshall Sklare, ed., *Understanding American Jewry* (New Brunswick: Transaction Books, 1982), 56–95.

11. See, for example, the series of papers published by the American Jewish Committee during the 1970s entitled *Jewish Education and Jewish Identity.* See also Jacob Neusner, *Stranger at Home: "The Holocaust," Zionism, and American Judaism* (Chicago: University of Chicago Press, 1981).

12. It might be argued that the Jewish religion is likewise a force determining Jewish identity. While obviously a very large proportion of modern Jews define their Jewish identity at least partially in religious terms, I understand the Jewish religion in the modern world to be an element of continuity, a given that reacts to external forces and is sometimes altered by them but is

Notes

not itself an impinging force. Thus Judaism during the last two centuries has been greatly influenced by enlightenment, somewhat affected by antisemitism, and certainly shaped by its response to Zionism. Even the divisions in modern Judaism—Orthodox, Conservative, Reconstructionist, and Reform—can be explained largely by the degree to which religious Jews of varying kinds have allowed enlightenment to influence their religious beliefs and rituals.

Enlightenment: *The Powerful Enticements of Reason and Universalism*

1. See especially Jacob Katz, *Exclusiveness and Tolerance* (New York: Schocken Books, 1961).

2. The most influential medieval Jewish legist, Moses Maimonides, wrote: "It is forbidden to praise them or even to say: How beautiful this idolator is in his appearance. So much the more so [is it forbidden] to speak in praise of his deeds or take to heart any of his words . . . for it causes one to become attached to him and to learn from his evil deeds" (*Mishneh Torah,* Hilkhot avodat kokhavim [Laws relating to idolatry], 10:4). (All translations here and elsewhere in these lectures are my own except where a published translation is cited in the notes.) That the category of idolatry included Christians (but not Muslims) is apparent from ibid., 9:4.

3. See, for example, the references to things Christian in the Hebrew Crusade chronicles. The original texts are in Adolf Neubauer and Moritz Stern, eds., *Hebräische Berichte über die Judenverfolgungen während der Kreuzzüge* (Hebrew reports on the persecution of the Jews during the Crusades) (Berlin: L. Simion, 1892). English translations for two chronicles are given in Robert Chazan, *European Jewry and the First Crusade* (Berkeley and Los Angeles: University of California Press, 1987), 225–97.

4. Haym Soloveitchik, "Three Themes in the *Sefer Hasidim*," *Association for Jewish Studies Review* 1 (1976): 311–57.

5. It is important to distinguish here between idea and identity. Even the Hasidic community was not hermetically sealed from the intellectual world of contemporary Christianity. Religious ideas penetrated medieval Jewish communities from the outside, in some instances creating parallel phenomena. But the adoption or adaption of a doctrine or a practice that has its origin outside the Jewish community does not necessarily entail identification with its source.

6. Schneur Zalman of Liadi, *Liqqutei amarim—Tanya* (Collected teachings), trans. Nissan Mindel (Brooklyn, 1962), 22–24.

7. For an abbreviated translation of Sofer's will see W. Gunther Plaut, ed., *The Rise of Reform Judaism* (New York: World Union for Progressive Judaism, 1963), 256–57.

8. A good example of such Jewish chauvinism is Meir Kahane's pamphlet entitled *Numbers 23:9* (Jerusalem, 1974).

9. Uriel Acosta, *A Specimen of Human Life,* trans. Peter M. Bergman (New York: Bergman Publishers, 1967).

10. Peter L. Berger has argued that heresy became the common condition in modernity once the "plausibility structure" of traditional beliefs was called into question and individual choice replaced the unquestioned acceptance of community authority. According to Berger, Jewish emancipation is "perhaps the most important example in the modern Western world" of this process. See his *The Heretical Imperative* (New York: Doubleday, 1979), esp. 29–30. The heretic is also a rebel and as such embodies an enduring characteristic of the culture hero in Western civilization. See O. B. Hardison, *Entering the Maze: Identity and Change in Modern Culture* (New York: Oxford University Press, 1981), 52–53. An allied concept to that of the Jew as heretic is the Jew as pariah, which, Hannah Arendt argued, Jewish poets, writers, and artists developed into a universal human type in the modern world. Such individuals were outsiders to both the Jewish community and the political and cultural consensus of the states in which they lived. See her *The Jew as*

Notes

Pariah: Jewish Identity and Politics in the Modern Age (New York: Grove Press, 1978), 67–90.

11. Isaac Deutscher, *The Non-Jewish Jew* (Boston: Alyson Publications, 1982), 25–27.

12. To be sure, there were underlying objective causes as well. For example, had not western and central European governments, eager to centralize and thereby strengthen their political and economic control, deprived Jews of the legal autonomy they possessed earlier, formidable barriers to outside identifications would have remained in place. But although such centralization drew Jews closer to non-Jews and political emancipation made them fellow citizens, I would argue that it was above all the more accepting attitude, derived from Enlightenment philosophy, that influenced Jews to reciprocate by regarding gentiles and what they stood for in a new and more open manner.

13. Moses Mendelssohn, *Jerusalem and Other Jewish Writings,* trans. Alfred Jospe (New York: Schocken Books, 1960), 89.

14. Geiger's early letters reflect what Erik Erikson called "the rage that is aroused wherever identity development loses the promise of a traditionally assured wholeness" and where anxieties are "aggravated by the decay of institutions which had been the historical anchor of an existing ideology" (*International Encyclopedia of the Social Sciences* [New York: Macmillan, 1968], vol. 7, s.v. "Identity, Psychosocial"). Geiger's letters were printed in *Allgemeine Zeitung des Judentums* 60 (1896): 52ff. I have given fuller interpretations of Hirsch, Frankel, and Geiger in my *Response to Modernity: A History of the Reform Movement in Judaism* (New York: Oxford University Press, 1988), 77–99.

15. This was true not only for professional Jewish scholars. Pauline Wengeroff, a Jewish woman who lived in Belorussia during the last half of the nineteenth century, wrote of her no-longer religious husband that he continued to study Talmud, "but this Talmud study wholly lost its earlier religious character and for my husband became more a matter of philosophizing, critical examination and investigation, and it no longer played the principal role in his life" (*Memoiren einer Grossmutter: Bilder aus der Kulturgeschichte der Juden Russlands im 19. Jahrhundert*

※

[Memoirs of a grandmother: Portraits from the cultural history of the Jews of Russia in the nineteenth century] [Berlin: M. Poppelauer, 1910], 2:114).

16. Lazarus Bendavid, *Etwas zur Charackteristick der Juden* (Something of the characteristics of the Jews) (Leipzig: J. Stahel, 1793), 45–53; Aaron Wolfssohn, *Jeschurun, oder unparteyische Beleuchtung der dem Judenthume neuerdings gemachten Vorwürfe* (Jeshurun, or an impartial examination of recent reproaches made against the Jews) (Breslau: no publisher, 1804), 111–16; and [Sabattia Joseph Wolff], "Status causae et controversiae in Sachen der Israeliten in Berlin die deutsche Synagoge betreffend" (Status of the cause and controversy in matters of the Israelites in Berlin with regard to the German synagogue), manuscript composed between 1812 and 1823 and published in *Leo Baeck Institute Year Book* 25 (1980): 111–30.

17. Isaac Baer Levinsohn's *Te'udah be-Yisrael* (A mission in Israel) was completed in 1823 but published only in 1828. There is a recent printing with an introduction by I. Etkes (Jerusalem: Zalman Shazar Center, 1977).

18. It could also be only one stage in a single adult life. Moses Leib Lilienblum, a prominent Russian Jewish writer, passed sequentially from darkest Orthodoxy to Haskalah and religious reform, on to positivism and socialism, and finally to Zionism.

19. Wengeroff, *Memoiren einer Grossmutter*, 2:134.

20. Abraham Ascher, *Pavel Axelrod and the Development of Menshevism* (Cambridge: Harvard University Press, 1972), 69–78, 339–40; Israel Getzler, *Martov: A Political Biography of a Russian Social Democrat* (Cambridge: Cambridge University Press, 1967), 27–29, 56–62.

21. See Zvi Y. Gitelman, *Jewish Nationality and Soviet Politics: The Jewish Sections of the CPSU, 1917–1930* (Princeton: Princeton University Press, 1972).

22. On Adler see Benny Kraut, *From Reform Judaism to Ethical Culture: The Religious Evolution of Felix Adler* (Cincinnati: Hebrew Union College Press, 1979).

23. During the late seventies there were about 1,200 *ba'ale teshuvah* studying in yeshivas in Jerusalem. Most of them came from the United States. See Janet Aviad, *Return to Judaism: Re-*

Notes

ligious Renewal in Israel (Chicago: University of Chicago Press, 1983).

24. *The Life and Soul of a Legendary Socialist: The Memoirs of Vladimir Medem,* trans. Samuel A. Portnoy (New York: Ktav, 1979), 129.

25. Franz Kafka, *Letter to His Father* (New York: Schocken Books, 1953), 78.

26. Walter Jens, "Ein Jude namens Kafka," in Thilo Koch, ed., *Porträts deutsch-jüdischer Geistesgeschichte* (Portraits of German Jewish intellectual history) (Cologne: M. DuMont Schauberg, 1961), 179–203.

Antisemitism: *The Ambiguous Effects of Exclusion and Persecution*

1. This is not, of course, equivalent to Jean Paul Sartre's extreme position that "it is the anti-Semite who *makes* the Jew" (italics in source) (*Anti-Semite and Jew* [New York: Schocken Books, 1948], 69). The French Jewish sociologist Georges Friedmann, while finding Sartre's position "penetrating but too simple," was nonetheless persuaded that an absence of antisemitism must profoundly alter the historically conditioned Jewish personality (*The End of the Jewish People?* [New York: Doubleday, 1967], 265–71).

2. Cf. Ben Halpern, "Reactions to Antisemitism in Modern Jewish History," in Jehuda Reinharz, ed., *Living with Antisemitism: Modern Jewish Responses* (Hanover, N.H.: University Press of New England, 1987), 4–6.

3. Yitzhak Baer, *A History of the Jews in Christian Spain* (Philadelphia: Jewish Publication Society, 1961), 1:237–42.

4. Cf. Z. Diesendruck, "Antisemitism and Ourselves," in Koppel S. Pinson, ed., *Essays on Antisemitism* (New York: Conference on Jewish Relations, 1946), 41–48.

5. Jewish jokes are one means of relieving the tension. They enable the teller to gain emotional distance from gentile stereotypes of the Jew through the device of ridicule. For some exam-

ples see Peter Gay, *Freud, Jews, and Other Germans* (New York: Oxford University Press, 1978), 209.

6. Celia Heller notes that in interwar Poland the Jewish assimilationists, who regarded Jewish characteristics as stigmata, "were so obsessed with Jewish traits as discrediting symbols that discovering the traits became a game in which they tried to outdo one another. Much of the gossip among them revolved around the Jewish signs that reappeared in others in unguarded moments, and around their discovery in people who had been hitherto successful in not revealing them" (*On the Edge of Destruction: Jews of Poland between the World Wars* [New York: Columbia University Press, 1977], 205).

7. Cited in Amos Elon, *Herzl* (New York: Holt, Rinehart & Winston, 1975), 66.

8. Erikson, *Identity: Youth and Crisis,* 60.

9. Typical is the old anecdote about an east European Jew, dressed in distinguishably Jewish clothing, who enters a train compartment and makes himself at home by putting his feet up on the cushion of the seat opposite his. When a fashionably dressed foreigner enters, the Jew immediately pulls back his dirty shoes and begs the gentleman's pardon. The newcomer then turns to him and says, "Are you travelling home for Passover?" Thereupon the first Jew, recognizing a coreligionist in the stranger, calmly puts his feet back on the seat and says, "*A zoi*" [something like: "so, okay"]. Cited from Theodor Lessing, *Der jüdische Selbsthass* (Jewish self-hate) (Berlin: Zionistischer Bücher-Bund, 1930), 30. Relevant also are these reflections set into a Hebrew short story by the east European maskil and early Zionist Perez Smolenskin:

What an amazing name is the name "Jew"! It has in its power instantly to turn joy into mourning, love into hate. In the homes of the nobility, enjoying themselves dancing and flirting with beautiful—and not so beautiful—women, everyone circulates about like close companions, brothers from the womb. And then suddenly there escapes from the mouth of one of them: "That man, he's a Jew!" As if there were terror all about, the expression on every face is changed, for this name was, is (and who knows whether it not also shall be?) a stumbling block for those who bear it, a dread and a horror to every gentile. He will eat with you, converse and do

94

Notes

business with you; he will give you his advice and ask yours—but all these only when he forgets who you are. If he recalls to what people you belong, all the brotherliness and love will vanish like smoke. But, on the other hand, on the lips of a fellow Jew this name has a magic quality: it removes all fear and fright from its hearer and often makes him forget even the feeling of respect that every man experiences toward one greater than himself. With love he draws in even persons who until now were complete strangers to him. (*Ha-Shaḥar* 5 [1873/74]: 570–71)

Such feelings persist even today among highly integrated American Jews. A survey of delegates to the 1985 Biennial Conventions of the Union of American Hebrew Congregations and National Federation of Temple Sisterhoods found that 62 percent agreed with the statement: "When I meet someone new, I personally feel more relaxed if that person is Jewish" (Mark L. Winer et al., *Leaders of Reform Judaism* [New York: Union of American Hebrew Congregations, 1987], 57).

10. A survey of Jewish students in southern California revealed more apathy toward their Jewish heritage than anxiety about it (Ronald Maury Demakovsky, "Jewish Anti-Semitism and the Psychopathology of Self-Hatred" [Ph.D. dissertation, California School of Professional Psychology, 1978]).

11. The Magen David is the six-pointed Shield of David, and *chai* is the Hebrew word for "lives" from the expression: "The people of Israel lives."

12. There is a large literature that bears on this subject. A recent major work, which however focuses almost exclusively on writers and especially on the shame induced by the unassimilated language of Jews, is Sander L. Gilman, *Jewish Self-Hatred: Anti-Semitism and the Hidden Language of the Jews* (Baltimore: Johns Hopkins University Press, 1986). A more general but far briefer treatment is Lionel Kochan, *Jewish Self-Hatred* (London: British Section, World Jewish Congress, 1970). Methodological issues are raised in Paul Morris and Alan Rosenberg, "Another Look at Jewish Self-Hatred," *Journal of Reform Judaism,* Summer 1989, 37–59. Still valuable is the brief essay by Kurt Lewin entitled "Self-Hatred among Jews," in his *Resolving Social Conflicts* (New York: Harper, 1948), 186–200. The term was first used by Theodor Lessing in *Der jüdische Selbsthass.*

13. Ironically, the man whom Marx especially liked to brand with Jewish epithets, his socialist rival Ferdinand Lassalle, was himself a despiser of fellow Jews. A student of Hegel, Lassalle adopted his mentor's view of Judaism. In 1844, the very year of Marx's "On the Jewish Question," Lassalle defined Judaism to his mother in strictly Hegelian terms: "The Jewish religion is the religion of harsh servitude under the abstract spirit, God." Later, in minimizing his Jewishness to a prospective Christian bride, he declared: "I do not like the Jews at all, I even detest them in general. I see in them nothing but the very much degenerated sons of a great but vanished past. During centuries of slavery, these men have acquired the characteristics of slaves, and that is why I am most unfavorably disposed towards them." Lassalle had found an example of such slave characteristics among the Jews accused of ritual murder in Damascus in 1840. He thought that they should have risen up violently against those who libeled them. It is another irony that later the Zionists would level similar charges of passivity against modern Jews. For the texts from Lassalle see Edmund Silberner, "Ferdinand Lassalle: From Maccabeism to Jewish Anti-Semitism," *Hebrew Union College Annual* 24 (1952–53): 151–86.

14. On Marx's negative Jewish identity see especially Edmund Silberner, "Was Marx an Anti-Semite?" *Historia Judaica* 11 (1949): 3–52, and Isaiah Berlin, "Benjamin Disraeli, Karl Marx, and the Search for Identity," *Midstream,* August/September 1970, 29–49.

15. I have used Stefan Grossmann's edition of Marx's "On the Jewish Question" (Berlin: Rowohlt, 1920). See especially pp. 40–49.

16. In psychoanalytic theory money is associated with excrement. Strangely, Marx finds it necessary to note that Jewish law even regulates conduct in the privy. Elsewhere he twice associates Jews with filth (Silberner, "Was Marx an Anti-Semite?" 32).

17. The most recent major study of Otto Weininger is Jacques Le Rider, *Le cas Otto Weininger: Racines de l'antiféminisme et de l'antisémitisme* (The case of Otto Weininger: Roots of antifeminism and antisemitism) (Paris: Presses universitaires de France, 1982). There is also a corrected and expanded German edition

Notes

(Vienna, 1985). Le Rider puts Weininger's ideas into their historical context, where they do not seem quite so strange. Yet historical influences offer only an incomplete explanation. For a defense of Weininger against application of the label "self-hating Jew," see Allan Janick, "Viennese Culture and the Jewish Self-Hatred Hypothesis: A Critique," in Ivar Oxaal et al., eds., *Jews, Antisemitism, and Culture in Vienna* (London: Routledge & Kegan Paul, 1987), 75–88.

18. Otto Weininger, *Geschlecht und Charakter*, 20th printing (Vienna: W. Braumüller, 1920), 402.

19. Ibid., 403–4.

20. "In the German speaking world Weininger was at that time one of the very few intellectuals who was dominated by a perhaps Christian and perhaps nihilistic pessimistic sentiment of the sinfulness of all life. Like most of such men he suffered from his self, the *moi haïssable*. This self-hatred turned against the two elements in his life that he thought responsible for the sinfulness of life and of his life: sexuality and Jewishness" (Hans Kohn, "Eros and Sorrow: Notes on the Life and Work of Arthur Schnitzler and Otto Weininger," *Leo Baeck Institute Year Book* 6 [1961]: 163). What bothered Weininger especially was that Jews refused to take guilt seriously. See his *Über die letzten Dinge* (Vienna: W. Braumüller, 1918), 177–78.

21. I have discussed this subject comparatively for England, France, and Germany in my "Ambiguity and Ambivalence: The Plight of Eighteenth-Century Jewry in Western Europe," in *Religion in the Eighteenth Century*, vol. 6 of the Publications of the McMaster University Association for Eighteenth-Century Studies (New York: Garland, 1979), 117–35.

22. *Philosophical Dictionary*, ed. W. Baskin (New York: Philosophical Library, 1961), 5:308–9.

23. [Isaac de Pinto], *Apologie pour la Nation Juive; ou, Reflexions critiques sur le premier chapitre du VII. Tome des Oeuvres de Monsieur de Voltaire, au sujet des Juifs* (Apology for the Jewish nation; or, Critical reflections on the first chapter of the seventh volume of the works of Mr. de Voltaire on the subject of the Jews) (Amsterdam: J. Joubert, 1762), 11–12, 17–19, 22. Excerpts from a nineteenth-century English translation are con-

tained in Paul R. Mendes-Flohr and Jehuda Reinharz, eds., *The Jew in the Modern World* (New York: Oxford University Press, 1980), 253–55.

24. Deborah Hertz, "Seductive Conversion in Berlin," in Todd M. Endelman, ed., *Jewish Apostasy in the Modern World* (New York: Holmes & Meier, 1987), 56–57.

25. Jonathan Frankel, "Crisis as a Factor in Modern Jewish Politics, 1840 and 1881–82," in Reinharz, ed., *Living with Antisemitism,* 51–55.

26. Allan Tarshish, "The Board of Delegates of American Israelites (1858–1878)," *Proceedings of the American Jewish Historical Society* 49 (1959/60): 16–32.

27. Todd M. Endelman, "Conversion as a Response to Antisemitism in Modern Jewish History," in Reinharz, ed., *Living with Antisemitism,* 59–83.

28. Moritz Lazarus, *Unser Standpunkt: Zwei Reden an seine Religionsgenossen am 1. und 16. December 1880* (Berlin: Stuhr, 1881), 11.

29. See my "Great Debate on Antisemitism: Jewish Reaction to New Hostility in Germany, 1879–1881," *Leo Baeck Institute Year Book* 11 (1966): 137–70.

30. The literature on the Centralverein deutscher Staatsbürger jüdischen Glaubens is large. On its early years see Ismar Schorsch, *Jewish Reactions to German Anti-Semitism, 1870–1914* (New York: Columbia University Press, 1972); Jehuda Reinharz, *Fatherland or Promised Land: The Dilemma of the German Jew, 1893–1914* (Ann Arbor: University of Michigan Press, 1975); Marjorie Lamberti, *Jewish Activism in Imperial Germany: The Struggle for Civil Equality* (New Haven: Yale University Press, 1978); and Sanford Ragins, *Jewish Response to Anti-Semitism in Germany, 1870–1914* (Cincinnati: Hebrew Union College Press, 1980).

31. Landgerichtsrath Wollstein, "Unser Verhalten gegen den Antisemitismus in politischer, sittlicher, und gesellschaftlicher Beziehung" (Our activity against antisemitism in relation to politics, morals, and society), *Im deutschen Reich* 6 (1900): 191.

32. In the mideighties Austrian Jews responded to native antisemitism by establishing the Österreichisch-Israelitische Union.

Notes

Like the Centralverein, which was founded almost a decade later, the union sought to instill Jewish pride and soon concentrated its activities on Jewish defense. See Marsha L. Rozenblit, *The Jews of Vienna, 1867–1914: Assimilation and Identity* (Albany: State University of New York Press, 1983), 153–58; Jacob Toury, "Troubled Beginnings: The Emergence of the Österreichisch-Israelitische Union," *Leo Baeck Institute Year Book* 30 (1985): 457–75. Jews in the United States created the American Jewish Committee in 1906 to safeguard Jewish rights following the Russian pogroms of 1903 and 1905. The committee, the Anti-Defamation League of B'nai B'rith (founded in 1913), and the American Jewish Congress (established permanently in 1922) were all responses to the persistence and resurgence of antisemitism in the twentieth century both in the United States and abroad. All have served as an ongoing identity focus for large numbers of American Jews, some of them not otherwise active in Jewish life.

33. Michael R. Marrus, *The Politics of Assimilation: A Study of the French Jewish Community at the Time of the Dreyfus Affair* (Oxford: Oxford University Press, 1971).

34. Cited in Fritz Stern, *Dreams and Delusions: The Drama of German History* (New York: Alfred A. Knopf, 1987), 74.

35. See Gay, *Freud, Jews, and Other Germans,* 101–8.

36. Moshe Ungerfeld, *Bialik ve-sofre doro* (Bialik and the writers of his generation) (Tel-Aviv: Devir, 1974), 155.

37. Herbert A. Strauss and Kurt R. Grossmann, eds., *Gegenwart im Rückblick: Festgabe für die jüdische Gemeinde zu Berlin 25 Jahre nach dem Neubeginn* (The present in retrospect: Jubilee volume for the Jewish community of Berlin 25 years after its new beginning) (Heidelberg: Lothar Stiehm Verlag, 1970), 231–47.

38. Ernst Simon, *Aufbau im Untergang: Jüdische Erwachsenenbildung im nationalsozialistischen Deutschland als geistiger Widerstand* (Construction on the eve of destruction: Jewish adult education in National Socialist Germany as spiritual resistance) (Tübingen: J. C. B. Mohr, 1969); Herbert Freeden, *Jüdisches Theater in Nazideutschland* (Jewish theater in Nazi Germany) (Tübingen: J. C. B. Mohr, 1964); the essays in *Leo Baeck Institute Year Book* 1 (1956): 68–162; and those in Arnold Paucker,

✤

ed., *The Jews in Nazi Germany, 1933–1943* (Tübingen: J. C. B. Mohr, 1986).

39. Yerachmiel Cohen, "The Jewish Community of France in the Face of Vichy-German Persecution," in Frances Malino and Bernard Wasserstein, eds., *The Jews of Modern France* (Hanover, N.H.: University Press of New England, 1985), 181–204.

40. Jean Améry, "On the Necessity and Impossibility of Being a Jew," in Anson Rabinbach and Jack Zipes, eds., *Germans and Jews since the Holocaust* (New York: Holmes & Meier, 1986), 80–96.

41. Shmuel Ettinger, *Ha-antishemiyut ba-et ha-ḥadashah* (Antisemitism in the modern age) (Tel-Aviv: Sifriyat Po'alim, 1978), 252–53.

42. The sociologist Nathan Glazer relates that when he recently expressed doubt about the future of Judaism in America but maintained that American Jews were politically secure, he was widely misunderstood. His pessimism about Jewish life in America, it was believed, could only be prompted by fears regarding antisemitism (*"American Judaism* Thirty Years After," *American Jewish History* 77 [1987]: 283).

Zion: *The Centripetal Force of Jewish Peoplehood*

1. On the difficulty of determining a single Zionist identity, see now especially Ehud Luz, *Parallels Meet: Religion and Nationalism in the Early Zionist Movement, 1882–1904* (Philadelphia: Jewish Publication Society, 1988).

2. Stephen M. Poppel, *Zionism in Germany, 1897–1933: The Shaping of a Jewish Identity* (Philadelphia: Jewish Publication Society, 1977), 85–92.

3. Some religious thinkers, especially in the United States, did admire Ahad Ha-Am and embraced his broad conception of Jewish culture. However, Solomon Schechter, the leading figure in Conservative Judaism at the beginning of the century, stopped

Notes

short of agreeing that a secularist could be as good a Jew as a religionist. Mordecai Kaplan, the founder of Reconstructionism, eventually declared Judaism a *religious* civilization, using a qualifying adjective that Ahad Ha-Am would not have allowed. See the discussion in Evyatar Friesel, "Ahad Ha-Amism in American Zionist Thought," in Jacques Kornberg, ed., *At the Crossroads: Essays on Ahad Ha-Am* (Albany: State University of New York Press, 1983), 133–41.

4. Simon Dubnow, *Nationalism and History,* ed. Koppel Pinson (Philadelphia: Jewish Publication Society, 1958), 89.

5. Dubnow held that the Jewish national will would have to manifest itself first in the Diaspora, else there would be no assurance of cultural efflorescence in the land of Israel. He wrote, "Only after we realize that the national will is able to persist in all the lands of our dispersion and there strengthen the centers of our nation, shall we be able to believe that it will also release the striving to build a cultural center for a portion of the nation in the land of Israel and to work for its firm establishment and significant influence on the lands of the Diaspora" (*He-Atid* 4 [1912]: 117).

6. Menahem Brinker, "Brenner's Jewishness," *Studies in Contemporary Jewry* 4 (1988): 234–35.

7. Max Nordau in *Die Welt,* 11 June 1897. Cited in Shmuel Almog, *Zionism and History* (New York: St. Martin's Press; Jerusalem: Magnes Press, 1987), 95.

8. Max Nordau in *He-Atid* 4 (1912): 208. Cf. Eliezer Ben-Yehuda in ibid., 92.

9. Nahum Sokolow, ibid., 147.

10. Joshua Thon, ibid., 128, 130. Thon, a rabbi, was not one of the Zionist radicals. Martin Buber expressed a similar racial conception of Jewishness about the same time. See his "Judaism and the Jews" (1909) in *On Judaism* (New York: Schocken Books, 1967), 17–18.

11. Ahad Ha-Am's essay on Leon Pinsker in *Al parashat derakhim* (On the crossroads), ed. Jeremiah Frankel (Tel Aviv: Devir, 1959), 69.

12. A. B. Yehoshua, *Between Right and Right,* trans. Arnold Schwartz (New York: Doubleday, 1981), 130.

13. "The Israeliness that [Israeli Jews] feel is, to a large extent, a special kind of Israeli identity—one that connects them only with those Israelis who are also Jews" (Arnold Lasker, "A Question of Identity," *Forum* 44 [Spring 1982]: 65).

14. Seif a-Din Zu'abi, cited in Rafik Halabi, *The West Bank Story: An Israeli Arab's View of Both Sides of a Tangled Conflict* (New York: Harcourt Brace Jovanovich, 1981), 244.

15. Those Israelis of Jewish origin who most sought to cut ties with Judaism and with that portion of the Jewish people that continues to live outside the land have found even the designation *Israeli* too Jewish and have chosen other identities instead, especially *Canaanite*. See, most recently, James S. Diamond, *Homeland or Holy Land? The "Canaanite" Critique of Israel* (Bloomington: Indiana University Press, 1986).

16. Shlomit Levy and Eliyahu Louis Guttman, *Arakhim va-amadot shel ha-no'ar ha-lomed be-Yisra'el* (Values and positions of schoolchildren in Israel), 2 vols. (Jerusalem: Institute of Applied Social Research, 1974–76), 1:10; Simon Herman, *Jewish Identity: A Social Psychological Perspective* (Beverly Hills: Sage Publications, 1977), 136–37.

17. Shlomit Levy and Eliyahu L. Guttman, "The Jewish Identification of Israelis in the Midst of the Yom Kippur War" (in Hebrew), *Bi-Tefutsot Ha-Golah* 67/68 (Winter 1973 [1974]): 50.

18. Thus A. B. Yehoshua defines the contemporary Zionist, whether living in Israel or abroad, as "a person who accepts the principle that the State of Israel belongs not only to its citizens but also to the entire Jewish people" (*Between Right and Right,* 123).

19. Karmi Yogev, a well-known Israeli educator, expressed it this way during an Israeli-Diaspora dialogue in 1969:

In noting that the past must remain a prime aspect of education, I should add that greater emphasis should be laid on our more, if you will, normal periods of history: the First Temple, the Second Temple, the colonization of Palestine in the past few generations. The younger generation is much more inspired by heroism and triumphs than by disasters. But we cannot overlook that the history of our people is, in very great part, a history of catastrophe, a history of disaster, a history of a people who had no means of defending them-

Notes

selves. The Israeli young tend to find these aspects of our negative history, to put it mildly, uninspiring. How to reach them on this score remains a problem. (*Congress Bi-Weekly*, 3 April 1970, 53)

20. Levy and Guttman, *Arakhim va-amadot*, 2:16.

21. Emanuel Guttman, ed., *Mishtar medinat Yisra'el: Sefer mekorot* (The governing system of the state of Israel: A book of sources) (Jerusalem: E. Kaplan School, 1971), 16.

22. Simon N. Herman, *Israelis and Jews: The Continuity of an Identity* (Philadelphia: Jewish Publication Society, 1971), 49.

23. Ibid., 52–53. An advertisement placed by the Israel Aliyah Center in the *Canadian Jewish News* (April 1975) began as follows: "We don't promise you a rose garden in the promised land. And all we can promise you is that you get a chance to live your life the way you want to live it. Even if you are Jewish. And about being Jewish, here in Israel that's something you forget about. We promise you that. Because nearly everyone here is."

24. Aharon Yadlin, *Hamarkiv ha-Yehudi ba-ḥinukh be-Yisra'el* (The Jewish component in education in Israel) (Jerusalem: Institute for Contemporary Jewry, Hebrew University, 1978), 22.

25. Herman, *Israelis and Jews*, 112.

26. Levy and Guttman, *Arakhim va-amadot*, 2:243.

27. This situation may be changing as more and more Israelis, including those of Afro-Asian descent, now have close relatives that migrated to America during the last decade. New York is no longer as strange to Israelis from Morocco or Iraq as it was earlier in Israel's history.

28. Levy and Guttman, *Arakhim va-amadot*, 2:120–21; Hanoch Smith, *Attitudes of Israelis towards America and American Jews* (New York: American Jewish Committee, 1983), 15.

29. Charles Liebman, "The Present State of Jewish Identity in Israel and the United States," *Forum* 27 (1977): 25.

30. Shlomit Levy, "Components of the Jewish Identity as Motivators for Jewish Identification among Jewish Youth and Adults in Israel in the Period 1967–1982" (in Hebrew) (Ph.D. dissertation, Hebrew University, 1985).

31. Eliezer Schweid, *Israel at the Crossroads*, trans. Alton Meyer Winters (Philadelphia: Jewish Publication Society, 1973), 187, 209; Gideon Aran, "A Mystic-Messianic Interpretation of

✴

Modern Israeli History: The Six Day War as a Key Event in the Development of the Original Religious Culture of Gush Emunim," *Studies in Contemporary Jewry* 4 (1988): 263–64.

32. Cited in Aran, "A Mystic-Messianic Interpretation of Modern Israeli History," 272. Yet also seen as Jewish, usually in a negative sense, are the *haredim,* the most traditional of Israeli Jews, who refuse to serve in the Israeli army.

33. Simon N. Herman, "Criteria for Jewish Identity," in Moshe Davis, ed., *World Jewry and the State of Israel* (New York: Arno Press, 1977), 170.

34. A. B. Yehoshua in *Musaf Ha-Arets,* 15 April 1983, 6.

35. Zvi Sobel, *Migrants from the Promised Land* (New Brunswick: Transaction Books, 1986), 11, 56; Moshe Shokeid, *Children of Circumstances: Israeli Emigrants in New York* (Ithaca: Cornell University Press, 1988), 20. Paul Ritterband has recently argued that the numbers in New York are somewhat smaller than usually calculated and that the percentage of Orthodox Jews among them is higher. See his "Israelis in New York," *Contemporary Jewry* 7 (1986): 113–26.

36. Literally, "those who descend" (singular, *yored*) as opposed to *olim,* "those who ascend" by immigrating to Israel.

37. Sobel, *Migrants from the Promised Land,* 209.

38. One survey showed that 84 percent of the respondents were in favor of returning, but few had made definite plans for their return (*American Jewish Year Book* 80 [1980]: 60).

39. Linda G. Levi, "Israelis in New York and the Federation of Jewish Philanthropies: A Study of Anomie and Reconnection," *Contemporary Jewry* 7 (1986): 167–80.

40. Shokeid, *Children of Circumstances,* 55–70, 207.

41. Ibid., 132.

42. Steven M. Cohen, *American Modernity and Jewish Identity* (New York: Tavistock, 1983), 158.

43. Hans Mol, *Identity and the Sacred: A Sketch for a New Social-Scientific Theory of Religion* (New York: Free Press, 1976), 266.

44. What Erikson writes about maturation is enlightening for the role of this rite of passage in Judaism:

Identity formation . . . arises from the selective repudiation and mutual assimilation of childhood identifications and their absorption in

Notes

a new configuration, which, in turn, is dependent on the process by which a society (often through subsocieties) identifies the young individual, recognizing him as somebody who had to become the way he is and who, being the way he is, is taken for granted. The community, often not without some initial mistrust, gives such recognition with a display of surprise and pleasure in making the acquaintance of a newly emerging individual. For the community in turn feels "recognized" by the individual who cares to ask for recognition. (*Identity: Youth and Crisis,* 159–60)

45. This is a ritual of recent origin, not universal but increasingly popular.

46. Simon N. Herman, "American Jewish Students in Israel," *Jewish Social Studies* 24 (1962): 15.

47. See Steven M. Cohen, *Ties and Tensions: The 1986 Survey of American Jewish Attitudes toward Israel and Israelis* (New York: American Jewish Committee, 1987); idem, *Ties and Tensions: An Update* (New York: American Jewish Committee, 1989).

48. The standard guide for Jews by Choice, produced for the Reform movement by a convert—Lydia Kukoff, *Choosing Judaism* (New York: Union of American Hebrew Congregations, 1981)—gives no attention to the new Jew's relation either to the Holocaust or to the state of Israel.

49. Yet Herman's study of Israeli students showed that only 28 percent of those surveyed thought that conversion to the Jewish religion without the sense of belonging to the Jewish people was sufficient to classify someone as a Jew (*Israelis and Jews,* 93).

Index

❧

Abuya, Elisha ben, 15
Acosta, Uriel, 14–16
Adler, Felix, 28
Afro-Asian Jews, 74, 81,
103*n27*
Ahad Ha-Am, 63–67, 70, 79,
100–101*n3*
Alliance Israélite Universelle,
48
American Jewish Committee,
88*n11*, 99*n32*
American Jewish Congress,
99*n32*
Améry, Jean, 56
Amsterdam: Jews of, 14–15
Anti-Defamation League of
B'nai B'rith, 99*n32*
Antisemitism, instances of:
Germany, 47; Damascus
Affair, 47, 96*n13*; Dreyfus
Affair, 52; Mortara Affair,
48; pogroms in eastern
Europe, 49; Nazism as
most extreme form of, 55
Arendt, Hannah, 90*n10*
Ashkenazi Jews: in de Pinto's
writings, 44
Auschwitz, 56
Auto-emancipation, 67
Axelrod, Pavel, 26

Ba'ale teshuvah, 29, 92*n23*
Bar/Bat Mitzvah, 80
Bar-Kokhba, Simeon, 68
Ben-Yehuda, Eliezer, 68
Berdyczewski, Micha Josef,
67
Berger, Peter L., 90*n10*
Bialik, Hayyim Nahman, 22,
54
Bloch, Joseph, 37
Board of Delegates of Ameri-
can Israelites, 48
Brandeis, Louis, 63
Buber, Martin, 3–4, 101*n10*
Bund (General Union of Jew-
ish Workers), 30, 64

Canadian Jewish News,
103*n23*
Central Association of Ger-
man Citizens of the Jewish
Faith, 23, 51
Cohen, Archbishop Theodor,
of Olmütz, 37
Communist Party, Jewish
Sections, 27
Conversion from Judaism,
12, 26, 34–35, 40, 46
Crémieux, Adolphe, 48
Crusade chronicles, 89*n3*

Index

and, 72; Israelis' heightened sense of, at times of isolation, 75; in Diaspora, 80; and sense of Jewish peoplehood, 84; and support for defense organizations, 84
Identity, Zionist: political, 62–64; cultural, 63; importance of language for, 68; roots in land, 68
Identity formation, 104–5n44
Intermarriage, 57
Israel, as designation of a people, 70
Israel, state of: produces decreased sensitivity to opinions of gentiles, 38; role of Jewish religion in as perceived by Herzl, 62; questions of identity caused by creation of, 70; religious Jews in, 73; secular Jews in, 73–74; struggle against Arabs as identity factor, 75; emigration from, 76–77
Israel Aliyah Center, 103n23
Israeli, as identity, 70–71

Jerusalem, 60
"Jews by Choice," 81–82, 84, 105n44
Jokes, 93–94n5
Judea and Samaria, 72, 76

Kafka, Franz, 30–32
Kaplan, Mordecai, 101n3
Katz, Jacob, 11

Kaufmann, Walter, 15
Kohn, Hans, 97n20

Lassalle, Ferdinand, 96n13
Lavater, Johann Caspar, 45
Law, Jewish, 12
Law of Return, 73
Lessing, Theodor, 95n12
Levinsohn, Isaac Baer, 23–24, 92n17
Liberal Judaism, 18
Liebermann, Max, 53–55
Lilienblum, Moses Leib, 92n18
Luxemburg, Rosa, 27, 30

Maccabees, 67
Maimonides, Moses, 24; his *Mishneh Torah*, 89n2
Marranos, 14
Martov, Julius, 26
Marx, Karl, 15; "On the Jewish Question," 39–40, 96nn13,14,16
May Laws, 49
Medem, Vladimir, 29–30, 32
Mendelssohn, Moses, 17, 19, 22, 35; response to Lavater, 45
Messianism, Jewish, 60
Mission of Israel, 18, 28, 60
Montefiore, Moses, 47
Mortara Affair. *See* Antisemitism, instances of
Mosaist, 21

Name changes among Jews, 37

109

Napoleon, 46, 52
Narodniki, 27
Nazism, 52, 53
Neo-Orthodoxy, 18, 47
Nietzsche, Friedrich, 66
Nordau, Max, 67

Österreichisch-Israelitische
Union, 98–99n32
Ostjuden, 31, 50

Pale of Settlement, 46, 64
Philo of Alexandria, 11
Pinsker, Leon, 67, 70
Pinto, Isaac de, 43–44

Reform Judaism, 27, 29, 47

Sartre, Jean Paul, 93n1
Scapegoats, 50
Schechter, Solomon, 100–
    101n3
Self-designations of Jews, 21
Self-hatred among Jews, 39–
    43; survey of literature on,
    95n12
Sephardi Jews: of Amster-
    dam, 14; as enlightened
    Jews, 24, 43–45; attitudes
    to Ashkenazi Jews, 45; in
    Israel, 75
Shelilat ha-golah, 77
Shoah. See Holocaust
Six-Day War, 75, 82
Smolenskin, Perez, 94n9
Socialists, Jewish: in eastern
    Europe, 26–27; messianic
    vision of, 60; as members
    of Bund, 64

Sofer, Moses, 13
Sokolow, Nahum, 68
Soloveitchik, Haym, 12
Soviet Union: Jewish revival
    in, 57; Jews in, 79–80
Spinoza, Baruch, 15
Symbols: chai, 38, 95n11;
    Magen David, 38, 95n11

Taufjuden, 38
Tchernichovsky, Saul, 22
Thon, Joshua, 68–69, 101n10
Trotsky, Leon, 27, 30
Trotzjudentum, 50

Voltaire: attack on Jews by,
    43–44

Weininger, Otto, 40–43,
    96–97n17
Wengeroff, Pauline, 26, 91–
    92n15
Wissenschaft des Judentums, 47

Yehoshua, A. B., 76–77,
    102n18
Yogev, Karmi, 102–3n19
Yordim, 77–78

Zionism: virtues of, 54; as
    solution to "Jewish Ques-
    tion," 61; hope of Return,
    61; and character qualities
    of Jews, 66; and question
    of normalcy, 69; nature of,
    70; as taught in Israeli reli-
    gious school system, 72;
    and Israeli identity, 72–73
Zionists, 54, 61, 62–63, 65

110